The Rise of China in the Global Economy

The Causes & Consequences of China's Economic Growth for A Level & IB Geography

By Peter Lowe

Dear Josh,

Life-changing!

Enjoy it.

Best,

DALL

This Paperback Edition Published in 2020

Text copyright © Peter Lowe

Book Cover Image: Yuan on the map of China (Source: © Elkov Oleg | Dreamstime.com)

PD = Public Domain Images

OGL = Open Government Licensed Images

CC = Creative Commons Licensed Images
https://creativecommons.org/licenses/by/3.0/igo/
https://creativecommons.org/licenses/by/4.0/

Graphs: Designed by Matt Lowe

About the Author

Peter Lowe lives in Northamptonshire, England. He graduated with a BA (Hons) in Geography from the University of Southampton, and has taught Geography in both Independent and State Schools in the UK for the past 30 years. As a Head of Department for much of his career, he has had considerable experience in preparing students for Geography exams at GCSE and A Level.

His interest in the geographical dimension to conflict, development and globalisation, combined with his belief in the benefits provided by digital technologies to enhance learning, have led him to become an author and self-publisher of numerous electronic books. His iBook publications on 'The Causes and Geographical Impacts of War in Afghanistan' and 'The Rise of the BRICS in the Global Economy' were 'highly commended' at the Geographical Association Publishers' Awards.

This paperback version of 'The Rise of China in the Global Economy' is for teachers and students at school, college or university, as well as anyone else with an interest in the nature and impacts of China's economic, social and political development, and its role in the global economy.

www.geographydigital.com

Preface

China is rarely out of the news. Since the early 1980s, the country has emerged from economic ruin to become one of the world's economic giants. The spectacular rise of China is having far-reaching effects on the economies of every other nation. China's citizens have prospered from the country's economic growth, but also face significant human costs, none more so than from the deteriorating environment. Controversy and suspicion usually follow every move that China makes, exacerbated by the secrecy and censorship that still prevail under the ruling Communist Party. Recent tensions between China and the US over trade and technology threaten China's ambitions to reach the next level of development. So too will the global economic fallout from the coronavirus pandemic which disrupted supply chains and decimated business activity during 2020. The challenge for China is how to manage its economic recovery and ensure sustainable growth, since any further setback is likely to antagonise the population, and thereby threaten the stability of the country.

Contents

Chapter 1: The Emergence of China as an Economic Power

China's move to a market orientated economy has propelled the country from the status of a struggling and backward '**Low-Income Country**' (LIC) to a vibrant and successful '**Newly Industrialised Country**' (NIC) within the space of just three decades. This vast nation of 1.4 billion people has shaken off the legacy of old-style communism, to rise to a position that threatens to overhaul the existing world order. Despite enduring a bumpy ride in recent years, China appears to be driving the world economy. It remains the country of the moment, but whether the country can sustain its spectacular economic transformation, and join the club of advanced economies, remains to be seen.

Key reasons for growth:

Modernisation policies following the death of Mao Zedong in 1976, including improved relations with the West

Government investment in major infrastructure projects, such as the Three Gorges Dam and the Beijing Olympics

Travel restrictions eased, allowing more Chinese to be exposed to Western culture

Cheap labour, and a very large workforce, for unskilled and semi-skilled work

Less stringent labour laws and health & safety laws, lowering business costs

Company tax structure more favourable than other countries

Huge population, and an expanding middle class, creating a massive domestic market

Savings culture, allowing banks to lend money to Chinese businesses

Greater access to export markets following membership of the World Trade Organization in 2001

Domestic and international tourism growth, with attractions including 'The Great Wall', the 'Terracotta Army' and the 'Forbidden City'

The rapid development and modernisation of China's economy has been one of the most remarkable stories of the late 20th and early 21st centuries. China has managed to move 400 million of its own people out of **extreme poverty** and a further 450 million out of **moderate poverty**. In late 2010, China surpassed Japan's **Gross Domestic Product** (GDP) for the first time, with China's GDP reaching $6 trillion. Continued growth has seen a more than doubling of China's GDP to $14 trillion at the end of 2019. Representing 16% of today's global economy, China is the world's second-largest economy after the United States. More remarkably, its GDP growth is responsible for around one-third of global GDP growth. However, its GDP per person, at $10,276 in December 2019, remains considerably lower than any of the Group of Seven (**G7**) economies.

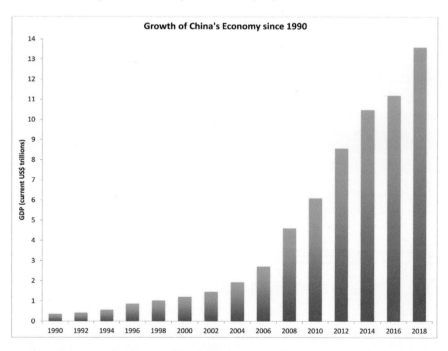

Growth of China's economy since 1990, measured by GDP in US$. Its GDP in 2019 exceeded $14 trillion. (Source: World Bank Data)

Unsurprisingly, China's involvement in world trade is significant. In 2018, it was worth more than $5.2 trillion, with exports valued at $2.66 trillion and imports costing $2.55 trillion. Its merchandise trade gave it a 13% share of global exports and 11% share of global imports. Both exports and imports increased on the previous year, giving China a trade surplus of around $110 billion. Nevertheless, its trade surplus has fallen in recent years, being a huge $320 billion less than it enjoyed in 2015.

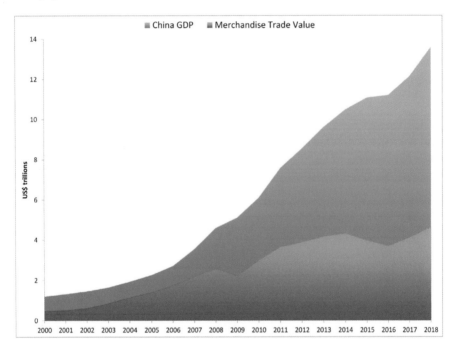

Changing value of merchandise trade in relation to the economy of China since 2000. The importance of trade is considerable, although it has weakened in recent years as the domestic economy has grown. (Source: World Bank Data)

1949-1979: Communism and the move towards a Market Economy:

China became a **communist country** in 1949, under the leadership of Mao Zedong, and for several decades there were few clues that this enormous country could mobilise itself into a world economic power. From 1950 to the late 1970s, the country remained an agricultural-based economy, with most production destined for the domestic market, and very little trade with the outside world. Nearly all industries were state controlled, and overseas investment was virtually non-existent. Under Mao, China's population grew from 550 million to more than 900 million. He saw China's large population in terms of economic strength (raising workers for the collective economy) and military strength (providing recruits for the People's Liberation Army). In reality, China was a poor country with a peasant economy unsuited to rapid population growth.

The Great Chinese Famine of 1959-1961 officially killed 15 million people, and possibly up to 40 million. Drought, poor weather and the failure of agricultural collectivisation as part of the '**Great Leap Forward**' policy of the Communist Party of China contributed to the famine. To make matters worse, Mao paralysed China further between 1966 and 1976 with the '**Cultural Revolution**' aimed at the repression and elimination of political opponents and capitalists. This attempt at strengthening communist ideology led to a period of virtual civil war, believed to be responsible for the deaths of between 0.5 and 2 million people, while also crippling the country's economy.

The death of Mao Zedong in 1976 provided an opportunity for right wing reformers in the Communist Party to win the power struggle for control of China. Deng Xiaoping, purged during the Cultural Revolution, emerged victorious in 1978, and started the process of moving China towards a **market economy**. The problems facing China were enormous. Population growth was out of control, infrastructure was poor, industry was hopelessly inefficient, and human capital was in short supply. The latter was due to the closure of universities, and suppression of intellectuals, during Mao's Cultural Revolution.

In 1979, the 'one-child' policy was introduced to tackle the acute **overpopulation** of China's rural areas, a major cause of poverty. Deng Xiaoping encouraged the selling of agricultural surpluses, through the Rural Household Responsibility System, with farmers allowed to keep any profits for themselves, and purchase more land to increase the potential for more wealth.

The 'One-Child' Policy:

Introduced in 1979, the policy was seen as essential in order to control poverty, prevent mass starvation (a feature during Mao's regime), and keep the total population below 1.5 billion, rather than it surging towards 2 billion. China's population size is the country's most important resource, and a major factor in its recent industrialisation, but overpopulation is a threat to sustainable economic growth.

*Chinese demographer, Liu Zeng, calculated in the 1980s that China's **optimum population** would be around 700 million in the 21st century. This is the population size which is most favourable for the level of resources and technology in the area. Overpopulation creates multiple problems in addition to famine. These include the growth of urban slums, high unemployment, lower living standards, pressure on schools and hospitals, as well as environmental degradation - air pollution, water shortages, contaminated water supplies, deforestation and soil erosion. Without the policy, the benefits of China's economic growth would have been spread too thinly.*

The 'one-child' policy helped to reduce the fertility rate from 2.9 in 1979 to 1.8 in 2009; reaching a low of 1.6 in 2016. The success claimed by the Communist Party was the prevention of 400 million births, keeping China's total population to a much more manageable anticipated peak of around 1.45 billion in 2029-2030 before falling steadily.

*The policy gave China the breathing space it needed to develop its economy through industrialisation and export-led growth, with Chinese workers becoming a valuable resource for state-owned and **transnational corporations** (TNCs) rather than a drain on resources. This 'demographic dividend' has helped the Chinese economy to grow by an average of 9% since 1990, with 400 million Chinese people lifted out of extreme poverty at the same time.*

The positive impacts are visible in the cities, where the policy became an accepted part of the Chinese lifestyle, and small family sizes allowed the purchase of more consumer goods, greater car ownership and longer holidays to be enjoyed. The financial rewards provided by the government, such as free education, life and medical insurance and pensions, have also been beneficial to families.

The negative impacts were felt more in the countryside, where resistance to the policy was far stronger, due to children being needed to help their families in the fields, and to provide for parents in old age. Tough enforcement by local government officials led to imprisonment, bullying and heavy fines (social compensation fees) for those who disobeyed the policy, as well as contributing to around 200 million sterilisations and 340 million abortions since the 'one-child' policy began. Many of these were the result of significant psychological, emotional and financial pressure applied to women by the authorities during a series of nationwide campaigns to enforce the rules.

The cultural preference for a son has been responsible for a noticeable gender imbalance in many parts of rural China, with around 120 boys for every 100 girls; a result of sex-selective abortions and even female infanticide. Across China, there are at least 30 million more young men than young women, creating the 'bachelor crisis'. In addition, 'hidden births' created millions of unregistered children lacking the entitlement throughout their lives of state benefits such as subsidised healthcare and education.

With increasing worries over the long-term implications of low population growth, China officially replaced the 'one-child' policy with a 'two-child' policy in 2016. It is hoped the relaxation in family size will mitigate the challenges facing China of a 'demographic time-bomb' resulting from a rapidly ageing population and a shrinking labour pool. In 2012, the working-age population peaked, and the number of dependents aged over 60 was 200 million (15% of the population), a number that is predicted to rise to 300 million in 2025 and 480 million by 2050.

Economic reforms were at the heart of Deng Xiaoping's policy-making. In 1979, diplomatic ties were re-established, and the door was simultaneously opened to foreign companies through China's first Joint Venture Law. This made it possible for overseas businesses to enter China, in partnership with local companies. Coca-Cola made its return to China in the same year, having been forced to leave in 1949.

1980s: Foreign Direct Investment and Special Economic Zones:

The first wave of **foreign direct investment** (FDI) involved investors from Hong Kong and Japan, attracted to low-cost manufacturing opportunities along China's east coast, particularly in the southern province of Guangdong. The **comparative advantage** of low wages offered by China's coastal provinces for overseas investors was reinforced by the establishment of **Special Economic Zones** (SEZs) from 1980. Initially, Shenzhen, Zhuhai and Shantou in Guangdong province, and Xiamen in Fujian province, became SEZs, offering foreign companies cheap land, tax incentives and high-quality infrastructure. Shenzhen's growth was particularly impressive, transforming itself from a group of fishing villages to a **megacity** in the space of a decade.

Growth & Importance of Guangdong Province:

Three of the four SEZs established by Deng Xiaoping in 1980 - Shenzhen, Zhuhai and Shantou - were based in the southern province of Guangdong. These SEZs were created with the intention of attracting FDI and encouraging China's private sector to develop its manufacturing capacity.

Deng Xiaoping's open-door policy radically changed the economy of the province as it was able to exploit its access to the South China Sea, proximity to Hong Kong, and historical links to the Chinese diaspora. Cheap and abundant land, inexpensive labour, relaxed regulations and a low rate of taxation provided further advantages compared to other provinces.

The designation of Shenzhen and Zhuhai as SEZs, both being situated in the Pearl River Delta (PRD) region of Guangdong, was a strategic move to act as an overflow opportunity for businesses based in Hong

Kong looking to expand their operations and reduce costs. Shenzhen boasts being the most important economic hub in Guangdong province today, with a focus on technology. Neighbouring Hong Kong remains a major economic powerhouse for the region, and a hub of international finance and services. Although its port is no longer important in shipping goods from mainland China, Hong Kong's stock market raises valuable capital for Chinese firms and around 60% of the FDI in China flows through the territory.

Guangzhou, the provincial capital that is also located in the PRD, has seen its economy grow rapidly as a global trading hub. With more than 108 million people, Guangdong is China's most populated province, while the PRD region is believed to be the world's largest urban area with a population exceeding 65 million.

Low-value-added manufacturing has typically characterised the province's economy since the 1980s. Labour-intensive industries, many of which are privately-owned, have attracted a huge migrant workforce. The huge output from factories producing electronics, domestic appliances, toys, clothing and footwear has ensured Guangdong's position as China's largest exporter of goods, accounting for at least 35% of the country's total exports in 2017, as well as the country's largest importer.

The PRD region, also known as the PRD Economic Zone, encompasses 9 heavily interconnected cities - Guangzhou, Shenzhen, Zhuhai, Foshan, Jiangmen, Zhongshan, Dongguan, Huizhou and Zhaoqing. The 2008-2020 plan for the economic zone has involved transitioning business activity away from basic assembly work to more advanced manufacturing and modern service industries. There has also been a concerted attempt to innovate in high-tech sectors, such as green energy, telecommunications, robotics, biomedicine and fintech. In addition, the plan has targeted growth in shipping, logistics, trade, conferences, exhibitions and tourism.

Since 2013, Shenzhen has allocated more than 4% of its annual GDP to R&D, putting it on a par with South Korea. Once notorious as a city of migrant workers and sweatshops, Shenzhen is now home to global tech companies, such as Huawei and Tencent. The aim is to further develop its knowledge-based economy. Achieving this will be facilitated by the 'Greater Bay Area' scheme, the central government's plan, announced in 2017, to link the 9 cities of the PRD Economic Zone with Hong Kong and Macau, creating an even more integrated economic and business hub. New transport infrastructure recently completed for the 'Guangdong-Hong Kong-Macau Greater Bay Area' includes the 55km long Hong Kong-Zhuhai-Macau Bridge and the Express Rail Link connecting Hong Kong to Shenzhen.

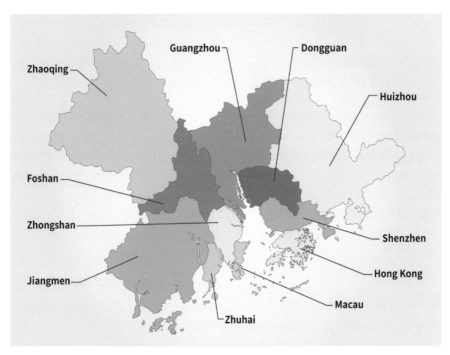

The 9 cities of the PRD Economic Zone are being integrated with Hong Kong and Macau to form the even larger 'Guangdong-Hong Kong-Macau Greater Bay Area'. (Image: © Kit Ying Ng | Dreamstime.com)

The success of Guangdong province is evident from its highly diversified economy which contributed $1.5 trillion to China's GDP in 2017, around 12% of the country's total. It has been the largest province by GDP since 1989, exceeding even the GDP of Australia which ranked, in 2017, as the world's 13th-largest economy. Economic growth, at 6.8% in 2018, was above the national average.

More SEZs and city-based **Economic and Technological Development Zones** (ETDZs), also referred to as 'open cities', followed from 1984. The ETDZs provided similar benefits for foreign investors as the SEZs, but had a greater focus on attracting technology rather than processing industries. Japanese investors continued to provide much of the infrastructure and technology needed by China, and in return Japan received shipments of the raw materials which its own industries required. At first, labour-intensive industries were set up, but later more advanced manufacturing plants were developed.

Attractions of China for Foreign Direct Investment:

Cheap and plentiful labour force for semi-skilled work

Large scale, modern and well-equipped manufacturing facilities, with the ability to upscale production very quickly to meet high demand

Hardworking mentality of the Chinese workforce, and limited restrictions on working hours

Encouragement from a supportive government, with fewer regulations, easier acquisition of land and lower taxes

Rapidly improving infrastructure, due to the Chinese government's huge investment in new roads, railways, ports, airports, telecommunications and electricity supply

Direct access to an expanding domestic market, as well as close proximity to the rest of the Asia region, and good access to North America via the Pacific Ocean shipping routes

China's dominant position in the global supply of rare earth metals, used in the telecommunications and consumer electronics industries

Special incentives in the Special Economic Zones (SEZs). Tax levied at 15% on production-orientated foreign investment

Similar reduced rates in the Economic and Technological Development Zones (ETDZs) created in many of the coastal cities

1990s: Shanghai and Transnational Corporations:

After the Tiananmen Square massacre of 1989, there were concerns that China might retreat from further economic liberalisation. However, Deng Xiaoping's promises of further reforms helped to dispel the fears of investors, and foreign investment in China shot up through the 1990s. Taiwan and the US, in particular, moved considerable capital into China and assisted Chinese companies with technical development.

Growth & Importance of Shanghai:

Located in the Yangtze River Delta area, Shanghai has been transformed, since gaining city status in 1927, to become China's key global city in its coastal core region. It is particularly important as a global commercial and financial centre, as well as being a major transport hub, home to the world's busiest container port. Its population is around 21 million.

Its emergence as an 'open city' began in 1986 with the establishment of the Minhang ETDZ in the city's suburbs. However, it was not until the 1990s that Shanghai took full advantage of Deng Xiaoping's blessing to the Chinese "to get rich", tripling in size in less than two decades. Under its mayor, Jiang Zemin, Shanghai made a remarkable transformation into a Western-style bold, glitzy and fashionable metropolis.

Shanghai is now a modern, sophisticated city, with a cosmopolitan character, and can boast a highly educated and skilled workforce, as well as being home to a higher proportion of affluent consumers than anywhere else in China. These factors have made it such an appealing destination for foreign investors.

The Pudong District, located along the east side of the Huangpu River, opposite the Bund waterfront area, is the commercial heart of Shanghai. It is dominated by its impressive skyscrapers (more than 100), symbols of the modern, progressive China. Its growth is linked to the establishment of the Pudong New Area (PNA) in 1993. The PNA is similar to the other SEZs in China, but it enjoys further preferential policies, such as allowing the establishment of foreign-owned financial institutions and their involvement in currency trading. In 2013, the government established a free-trade zone within the PNA as a pilot for further economic reforms.

Pudong District of Shanghai, on the east side of the Huangpu River. The impressive skyscrapers are clues to its important commercial and financial status. (Image: © Peter Lowe)

The western tip of the PNA is part of the Lujiazui Finance and Trade Zone, and acts as the main financial hub. The best-known buildings include the Oriental Pearl Tower, the Jin Mao Building and the Shanghai World Financial Center. The 632m tall Shanghai Tower is Pudong's tallest skyscraper, completed in 2015 at a cost of more than $2 billion.

The occupiers of Shanghai's impressive real estate are banks, insurance companies, fund management companies, futures companies, hotels and retail chains. Many are Western companies or joint Western-Chinese ventures, with the vast Chinese market being the main prize.

In 2017, Shanghai was home to around 1,500 financial institutions, with almost 30% involving foreign investment. The Shanghai Stock Exchange (SSE) opened in 1990, and is now the 4th largest exchange in the world by market capitalisation. It has more than 1,000 listed companies.

Heavy industries have also contributed significantly to Shanghai's growing economy, and include steel, shipbuilding and automobiles. China's largest steelmaker, Baosteel Group Corporation, is located in Shanghai. China's largest automobile manufacturer, the state-owned SAIC Motor Corporation, is also located in Shanghai, and enjoys partnerships with both Volkswagen and General Motors.

Per capita GDP for the residents of Shanghai has risen from under $1,000 in 1977 to $20,375 in 2018. The municipality's total GDP was $470 billion in 2017. Its economy has been growing at a faster rate than China as a whole, having recorded double digit growth for 15 consecutive years from 1992.

Shanghai is responsible for around 10% of China's exports of goods. It has attracted 25% of the FDI in China, much of it in the financial services sector. Manufacturing accounts for around 25% of Shanghai's GDP, with almost 70% coming from the service sector.

More than 500 foreign investors have their regional headquarters in Shanghai, and many of these have manufacturing facilities located there too. They include Exxon Mobil, General Electric, General Motors, Volkswagen, Intel, Siemens and Coca Cola.

One of the negative aspects from the rapid growth of Shanghai has been the considerable dislocation of its residents. More than a million households have been displaced to flats on the edge of the city, in order to make way for the massive commercial developments in the central zone. Booming property prices have also contributed to residents being forced to live further out.

Residential neighbourhood close to central Shanghai. The city is home to 21 million people, but booming property prices are forcing many residents to live further out. (Image: © Peter Lowe)

Around 4 million migrant labourers in the past 20 years have arrived in Shanghai, making up a quarter of the workforce. Many suffer from poorer living conditions than the locals, and with fewer rights to health or education.

The only thing likely to stop the continued growth of Shanghai is the Chinese Communist Party itself. The attempt to reduce regional disparities in income may see more attempts to push development further inland.

Through the 1990s, China invested roughly 9% of its GDP annually on infrastructure, helping to facilitate the expansion of the coastal belt. More SEZs and ETDZs were established, facilitating the growth of the country's manufacturing workforce. In 1993, Deng Xiaoping stated that "to get rich is glorious", and the people of China were quick to take advantage of the government's acceptance of capitalism. The young people, in particular, were glad of the opportunity to escape the rural poverty of their parents and grandparents, by migrating to the coastal areas to work in the new factories inside the SEZs.

Role of Coca-Cola in China:

Coca-Cola opened its first bottling plants in China, in the cities of Shanghai and Tianjin, in 1927. The company was forced to leave China following the Communist Revolution of 1949. It re-entered China in 1979, the first overseas company to grasp the opportunity arising from the 'open-door' policy of Deng Xiaoping.

Shanghai Shen-mei Beverage & Food Co. Ltd. is a joint venture operation with Coca-Cola. The bottling plant is one of the largest in Asia. (Image: © Peter Lowe)

Coca-Cola had 45 plants in China by 2017, and its sales accounted for around 15% of China's soft drinks market. It has invested in excess of $9 billion in the country since 1979, introducing more than 60 products under 20 brands. The company employs approximately 50,000 Chinese workers.

With the number of middle-class Chinese expected to increase considerably, and local tastes for drinks changing, Coca-Cola is poised to enjoy incredible sales growth. It invested an additional $4 billion between 2015 and 2017 to grab more of a share of the lucrative soft drinks market in China, valued at $84 billion in 2017. Its diversified product range includes a variety of juices, ready-to-drink tea and health-based drinks.

Coca-Cola will also benefit from McDonald's expansion in China, since it is the soft-drink supplier for each McDonald's location. McDonald's had 2,500 restaurants in China in mid-2017, and expects to open a further 2,000 by 2022.

TNCs were happy to take advantage of China's cheap labour, lack of trade unions, low company tax rates and large market potential, by moving their low and semi-skilled manufacturing facilities from the **High-Income Countries** (HICs) to China. Most factories were set up to assemble imported components into consumer goods for export, taking advantage of the incentive of zero tariffs on imports. TNCs were attracted by the comparative advantage of operations in China. For China, the benefits from this arrangement were earning money from exports, gaining access to technology, and increasing the skills of its workforce.

Further incentives for foreign investment in China came in 1991, shortly after the opening of the Shanghai Stock Exchange, when the government gave permission for some foreign banks to open branches in Shanghai, and allowed foreign investors to purchase shares in Chinese stocks. As China's economy grew, the country's increasing investment in education provided a growing pool of talented young Chinese, encouraging more foreign high-tech industries, including research and development facilities, to locate in the SEZs. In 2001, FDI in China reached over $40 billion.

Role of Apple in China:

China is a key manufacturing base for Apple, particularly for final assembly of the company's mobile devices. It is also a rapidly growing market for Apple's products. By 2017, China was generating 25% of all Apple's profits and was the company's second-largest market.

Apple's main outsourcing partners are Foxconn Technology Group, Quanta Computer and Pegatron Corporation. These companies, which are Taiwanese TNCs in their own right, also manufacture electronics for other companies, including Microsoft, Google, Hewlett-Packard and Dell. Their expertise in the assembly of consumer electronics products attracts the world's largest TNCs, such as Apple, to China. Foxconn's operations in China include its giant facilities at Shenzhen (Guangdong province) and Zhengzhou (Henan province), which assemble iPhones and iPads. Each factory complex employs up to 400,000 people when operating at full capacity, producing consumer electronic devices for Apple and many other TNCs.

*China's attractions for Apple include the low wages of its semi-skilled workers, the ability to scale production up and down faster than elsewhere, and its location at the heart of Apple's main **supply chain**. The availability of outsourcing partners from Taiwan takes away a significant part of the business risk for Apple, as the Taiwanese companies are responsible for building and operating the factories in China.*

Apple's iPhone 4 was assembled by Foxconn for just $7 per device, at its launch in 2010. However, outsourcing production to companies, such as Foxconn, does create risks for Apple, particularly as the company's success makes it a target for media scrutiny. Migrant workers account for 99% of the workforce, many are teenagers aged 17-19, and vulnerable to exploitation. Wages in 2010 were around $140 per month, but there were allegations that workers received as little as $2 per day, after deductions for meals and company dorms. Many were forced to work excessive overtime, often exceeding China's legal limit.

The bad publicity from 14 suicides, and numerous attempted suicides, at the Shenzhen plant, during 2009-2010, led to Apple initiating an investigation by the Fair Labor Association (FLA) into conditions at the *factory. In response to their report, health and safety procedures were strengthened, facilities for the workers improved, and wages were increased. By 2013, workers were receiving almost $700 per month before deductions for food and accommodation, nearly five times the 2010 level.*

Since 2013, Apple has been shifting its supply chain away from Foxconn to Pegatron, although claims of labour violations have continued. In 2014, a BBC investigation into conditions at Pegatron's iPhone 6 and iPad assembly plants, near Shanghai, claimed that workers were regularly exceeding 60-hour weekly limits, causing some to fall asleep during their shifts. Others had allegedly been forced to work for 18 days in a row, having been denied time off.

Apple responded to criticism of excessive working hours by claiming that it monitored the hours of more than a million workers in its supplier factories, and that they achieved an average 93% compliance with 60-hour working-week limits. Suppliers have been forced to compensate workers over excessive working hours and involuntary labour.

China has been a particularly lucrative market for the iPhone, made possible by Apple's deal in 2014 with China Mobile, the country's biggest carrier. Apple opened its first retail store in China in 2008, and by mid-2018 had 42 stores operational. Since 2015, Apple has sold more iPhones in China than in the USA, however China's economic woes, and competition in the smartphone market from Samsung, Huawei and Xiaomi, have hit iPhone sales more recently. In the third quarter of 2019, China accounted for 17% of Apple's total revenue, 10% less than in 2015.

Rising labour costs and the fallout from the ongoing US-China trade war, which began in 2018, have led to Apple exploring the possibility of shifting some of its iPhone production to other countries in South East Asia, particularly India and Vietnam. Any such move will jeopardise the estimated 5 million Chinese jobs believed to be dependent on Apple's manufacturing operations in China.

2000s: Three Gorges Dam and Chongqing:

The Three Gorges Dam project on the Yangtze River in Hubei province, was a key part of China's development drive. This $25 billion project involved the resettlement of at least 1.2 million people, and involved more than a decade of construction. The primary aim was to control flooding downstream, thereby reducing the levels of death and destruction which had plagued communities close to the river over many decades.

The Three Gorges Dam reduces the risk of flooding downstream for the settlements in the Yangtze River basin, an area that accounts for 40% of China's GDP. (Image: © Peter Lowe)

However, this **resource frontier** location would provide many other benefits. One of these was the provision of large amounts of 'pollution-free' electricity, equivalent to the output from 11 nuclear power stations, enabling China to meet the growing demand for power from the industrial cities of the coastal provinces.

Furthermore, it was hoped that access to cheap electricity would help to open up more of the nearby interior to FDI, thereby spreading wealth from the coastal provinces further inland. In addition, the regulation of the river's flow would facilitate easier shipments of raw materials and goods along the Yangtze, as well as enabling access to irrigation for farmers involved in cash crops production. By 2012 the dam was fully operational, with a reservoir stretching 600km through the scenic Three Gorges region.

Growth & Importance of Chongqing:

Located in the upper Yangtze River basin, Chongqing is both a city and municipality, once part of Sichuan province. It is China's largest inland port, and a key city in the country's 'Great Western Development Strategy', acting as a growth pole for the peripheral interior. Over time, it has developed into a secondary core area.

New settlements in the Chongqing municipality have been constructed at an impressive speed and scale alongside the reservoir of the Three Gorges Dam. 1.2 million people had to be resettled, due to the rising water. (Image: © Peter Lowe)

Chongqing now benefits from the electricity generated by the Three Gorges Dam. The dam has also allowed ships to reach the city's river port more easily. Over 8 million people live in the city itself, and around 32 million people are living in the wider urban region. Half a million migrant workers arrive each year.

Heavy Industries have played a major role in Chongqing's growing economy. These include iron and steel, aluminium, chemicals, textiles, machinery and automobiles. Southwest Aluminium (SWA), Asia's largest aluminium manufacturer, is located in Chongqing.

PetroChina, China's largest oil and gas producer, is constructing an oil refinery and new pipelines to process crude oil from north-west China, and potentially from Myanmar, the Middle East and Africa.

Other important industries are motorcycles, pharmaceuticals, electronics and food processing. Chongqing is China's largest centre for motorcycles, with more than 12 million produced each year. The automotive industry employs over 400,000 workers in the area. In total, manufacturing generates 40% of Chongqing's wealth.

An increasing number of foreign investors have been attracted to Chongqing, including BP, Barclays, Ford, Honda, Philips and Suzuki. The city is attempting to move up the value chain by attracting more high-tech and knowledge-intensive industries. Per capita GDP for the residents of Chongqing was $9,921 in 2018. Total GDP for the Chongqing Municipality was $286 billion in 2017.

From 2002 until 2016, Chongqing's economy grew at breakneck speed, enjoying double-digit annual growth. It was China's fastest-growing region in 2016, but growth has since slowed due to the scaling back of government investment in the face of mounting debts. The city's automotive industry declined in 2018 due to falling sales of budget models, while growth in the electronics sector was sluggish.

Chongqing is notorious for its poor air quality. High levels of sulphur dioxide from coal-burning industries have plagued the city for years. Nitrous oxide emissions from vehicles have increased recently too.

Central Chongqing visible on a relatively rare pollution-free night. The city has a population of more than 8 million, but around 32 million people live within the wider Chongqing municipality, of whom at least half are urban-based. (Image: © Bo Li | Dreamstime.com)

China's acceptance into the **World Trade Organization** (WTO) in 2001 was an important milestone for the country's involvement in global trade, allowing China to access more international markets, and giving overseas companies improved access to China's huge domestic market. Trade boomed from $266 billion of exports in 2001, to $969 billion in 2006. The government continued its massive investment in new roads, railways and airports, as well as telecommunications, to open up more of China, and ensure that its major cities had a world-class infrastructure.

By 2006, China was the world's largest recipient of FDI, with over $700 billion of foreign capital, and more than 500,000 joint ventures or wholly owned foreign enterprises. More than 50% of its exports were linked to FDI, and its economy grew by just over 10%.

Relationship between China's Development & TNCs:

China has been the world's production site since the growth of the SEZs. Without TNCs investing in their own production facilities in China, agreeing joint ventures or giving contracts to Chinese firms, the economic growth of the past few decades would not have materialised. Inbound investment (FDI) reached $142 billion in 2018 according to research by the UN.

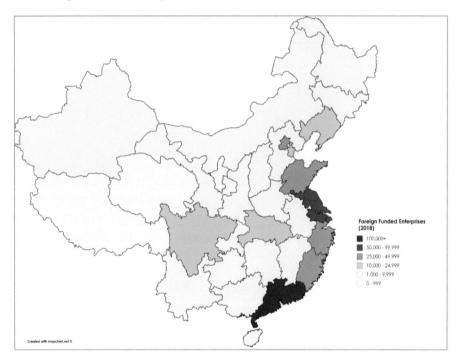

FDI has been hugely important to the economies of China's coastal provinces. The main recipient has been Guangdong province which was home to almost 171,000 foreign funded enterprises in 2018, nearly twice as many as Shanghai in second-place. At the other extreme, only 266 foreign funded enterprises were operating in Tibet. (Source: National Bureau of Statistics, China)

The TNCs have grown and benefited profitably from the lower production costs in China. Without TNC investment, China's economy would have grown at a much slower rate.

Asian companies are by far the biggest investors in China. Investment from the top 10 economies in Asia was valued at $102 billion in 2013.

However, China's reliance on TNCs is to some extent decreasing as Chinese companies mature, increase their own exports, and extend their influence abroad by becoming TNCs in their own right. China's outbound direct investment in 2018 reached $120 billion, an increase of $30 billion on its investment abroad in 2013. 57% of this investment came from privately-owned Chinese companies.

Chinese construction companies, automobile and motorcycle manufacturers, electronics firms, mining and energy companies are already exploiting the opportunities for global operations, and tapping into new markets.

In 2007, China's economy surpassed the $3 trillion mark, with an average per capita income of $2,200. It had become the 'factory to the world', producing most of the toys, electrical appliances, and consumer electronics that consumers worldwide demanded. Its exports grew to more than $1.2 trillion. China's focus on importing raw materials for further processing, and importing components for final assembly, meant that 60% of its exports were manufactured goods. The country could boast production of 90% of the world's toys, 60% of the world's bicycles, 55% of the world's shoes, and 50% of the world's computers.

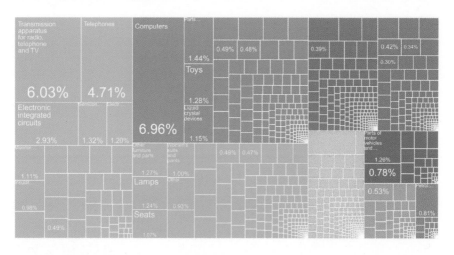

China's exports in 2016. Manufacturing, especially of electrical and electronics equipment, drives export earnings. (Source: © Atlas of Economic Complexity, CC)

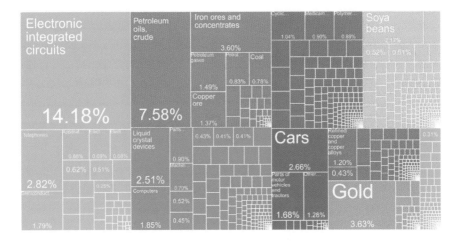

China's imports in 2016. Petroleum oils, other raw materials and components for manufacturers are significant. (Source: © Atlas of Economic Complexity, CC)

The success of China's economic expansion has not been without problems. Since 2007, it has had to deal with inflationary pressures in the economy. The huge inflow of capital from overseas has been one factor, but so has massive lending from the state-owned banks for investment projects. China runs a considerable **trade deficit** with suppliers of oil, iron ore and other commodities, such as Saudi Arabia and Australia. Its demand for food, raw materials and other goods has been growing at 10% a year.

On the flip side, it runs big **trade surpluses** with the US and many European countries. So, overall the country has prospered, with its economy contributing more than the US economy to world economic growth.

China's Trade in Goods with Selected Countries (2018)			
China-USA Trade	Exports $539 billion	Imports $120 billion	Surplus $419 billion
China-UK Trade	Exports $45 billion	Imports $23 billion	Surplus $ 22 billion
China-Germany Trade	Exports $120 billion	Imports $105 billion	Surplus $15 billion

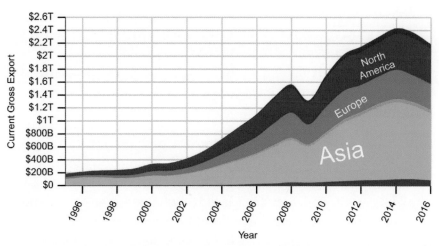

Changing significance of different world regions for China's exports since 1995. The increasing importance of Asia (especially East Asia) and North America as export markets is noticeable. (Source: © Atlas of Economic Complexity, CC)

2009-2020: Global Slowdown and Investment at Home:

Almost inevitably, China's boom years had to come to an end. Economic growth has been noticeably less rapid since 2009, mainly due to the effects of the 2007-2008 **Global Financial Crisis**. The global economic slowdown that followed led to many countries experiencing a long-lasting recession until 2012, resulting in falling demand for China's exports. Millions of Chinese workers had to be laid off. Although official unemployment figures have stayed below 5%, the country's vulnerability to events in the world's **advanced economies** has been clearly evident.

The response of the Chinese leadership has been to invest heavily, in both existing and new urban areas, and make credit easily available. $400 billion of direct government spending took place in just two years, and a surge in lending provided by the state-owned banks has ensured strong domestic demand. This has helped to soak up the effects of the slack global demand for China's products, allowing the economy to return growth figures between 6-7%, relatively healthy but still much lower than the double-digit growth rate levels seen before the Global Financial Crisis.

In fact, government expenditure has been essential in keeping the economy growing above 6% annually, a level widely regarded as the minimum to avoid discontent among the population. Nevertheless, much of the new development in the cities has been speculative and credit-driven, creating over-capacity which is unlikely to be sustainable in the long-term.

With industries worldwide struggling, it is perhaps unsurprising that criticism has grown regarding China's manipulation of its own currency, the renminbi (yuan). Exchange rate movements in China are tightly controlled, and this has led to what many see as an under-valued currency, lowering the cost of China's exports. In 2019, the US officially labelled China as a currency manipulator, in response to the yuan trading above the seven to the dollar mark, although it revoked its decision in January 2020 as part of a de-escalation of the US-China trade war. China has also faced accusations of '**dumping**' some of its goods in international markets. Furthermore, it is believed that China still does deals that are outside the rules of the WTO, such as selling weapons to African governments, in exchange for oil.

However, of far greater concern to both China and its international competitors in early 2020 was an outbreak of a new coronavirus (the SARS-CoV-2 virus and its disease COVID-19) which spread rapidly from the city of Wuhan, Hubei province. The new virus, responsible for acute respiratory infection in victims, is a close relative of the SARS coronavirus which emerged in China's Guangdong province in 2002, and cost the industry billions of dollars. The COVID-19 virus hit China's economy hard at the start of 2020. Factory output in February fell dramatically as manufacturers, retailers and offices across China were forced by the government to close their facilities to contain the spread of the virus. Millions of jobs were lost as China's economy contracted by 6.8% in the first quarter of the year. A gradual relaxing of restrictions during March saw factory output and exports begin to rise. However, reversing the contraction of the economy will be challenging as the worldwide spread of the COVID-19 virus quickly led to a coronavirus pandemic, causing a huge slump in global demand for many Chinese goods.

The Emergence of China as an Economic Power Concluded:

China's move to a market-orientated economy has propelled the country from the status, 40 years ago, of a struggling LIC to an established and powerful NIC in today's global economy. China accounts for one-third of global manufacturing, it is the world's largest exporter and the growth of its economy has been meteoric. The ability to supply cheap labour quickly has allowed companies to increase their production at a speed which other countries simply cannot match.

Inevitably, there have been trade-offs too. FDI in China reached a record $142 billion in 2018, providing millions of jobs for the Chinese workforce, but few taxes are being paid by companies in the SEZs, and profits leak out of China to the countries of origin of the TNCs. Imports have continued to grow rapidly, and the country's thirst for raw materials, including oil, is relentless. The coronavirus pandemic of 2020 will test the economic and political resilience of China's government and people. Yet, even as China's growth slows, it will continue to be a powerhouse for the global economy over the coming decades.

China in Numbers:

Population: 1.40 billion (2019)
Age Structure: 0-14 years 17.2%; 65+ years 11.3% (2018)
Median Age: 37.7 years (2018)
Dependency Ratio: 37.7% (2015)
Population Growth Rate: 0.37% (2018)
Birth Rate: 12.1 per 1,000 (2018)
Death Rate: 8.0 per 1,000 (2018)
Life Expectancy at birth: 75.8 years (2018)
Urban Population: 59.2% (2018)
Urbanisation Rate: 2.4% (annual average since 2015)
GDP: $14.38 trillion (2019)
GNI: $13.55 trillion (2018)
GNI (purchasing power parity): $25.26 trillion (2018)
GDP per capita: $10,276 (2019)
GNI per capita: $9,470 (2018)

GNI per capita (PPP): $18,140 (2018)
GDP Growth: 6.1% (2019) / GDP Decline: -6.8% (Q1 2020)
HDI: 0.752 (2017)
Gross National Saving: 46% of GDP (2017)
GDP by sector: Services 52%; Industry 40%; Agriculture 8% (2017)
Labour Force: 807 million (2017)
Labour Force by sector: Services 43%; Industry 29%; Agriculture 28% (2016)
Unemployment Rate: 5.9% (March 2020)
Population Below Poverty Line: 3.3% (2016)
Gini Coefficient/Index: 0.468 (2018)
Inflation Rate: 1.6% (2017)
Public (Government) Debt: 47% of GDP (2017)
External (Government & Private) Debt: $1.60 trillion (2017)
Reserves of Foreign Exchange & Gold: $3.24 trillion (2017)
Exports: $2.66 trillion (2018)
Main Export Partners: USA 18%; Hong Kong 14%; Japan 6%; South Korea 5% (2016)
Imports: $2.55 trillion (2018)
Main Import Partners: South Korea 10%; Japan 9%; USA 9%; Germany 5% (2016)

(Data Source: World Bank & Central Intelligence Agency/US Gov, PD; some 2019 figures subject to recalculation)

Quick Questions:
- *How does China's GDP per person compare with the G7 economies?*
- *What was valued at more than $5.2 trillion in 2018?*
- *Between which years was Mao Zedong the leader of China?*
- *Which leader began reforming China along the lines of a market economy?*
- *Why was the 'one-child' policy introduced?*
- *What have been the economic benefits of the 'one-child' policy?*
- *What might be viewed as the economic negatives of the 'one-child' policy?*
- *Which area of China was first to take advantage of the new Joint Venture Law?*
- *What are the attractions of the SEZs for foreign investors?*
- *What advantages did Guangdong province offer for businesses over other provinces on China's east coast in the 1980s?*
- *How has Shenzhen transformed itself in recent years?*
- *What is the purpose of the 'Greater Bay Area' scheme?*
- *From which two countries did investors move into China, at a significant rate, during the 1980s and 1990s?*
- *What evidence illustrates the importance of financial services to the*

economy of Shanghai?
- *Why has not everyone in Shanghai benefited from the city's economic boom?*
- *Why has Coca-Cola increased its investment in China in recent years?*
- *What are China's main attractions for Apple?*
- *How many people are employed by Chongqing's automotive industry?*
- *To what extent is the growth of Chongqing a 'mixed blessing'?*
- *When was China accepted into the World Trade Organization?*
- *What was the significance of 2006 for FDI in China?*
- *Give two statistics that illustrate China's important role in manufacturing.*
- *What has been the Chinese government's response to the global economic slowdown?*
- *What are the criticisms, usually made by other governments, regarding China's currency?*

Tasks & Discussion:
- *Produce three fact files showing the economic roles and importance of Guangdong, Shanghai and Chongqing.*
- *Which location is the most important globally and why? Which location is the least important globally and why?*
- *Describe fully the transformation of China from a LIC to a NIC economy, including the role of the government in this change.*
- *Explain the attractions of China for FDI, such as the investment by Apple & Coca-Cola in the country.*
- *How has the Chinese government ensured economic growth, despite the 2007-2008 Global Financial Crisis?*
- *Discuss the importance of China in today's global economy.*

Chapter 2: Regional Development and Inequality in China

Prior to 1978, strong centralised control over resource distribution ensured fewer inequalities between China's urban and rural societies, and between coastal and interior regions. For example, raw materials were processed within the regions where they were extracted, which tended to favour the interior. Equally, restrictions on rural to urban migration prevented the loss of talent from the countryside, as well as stopping the development of large shanty towns in the cities. Under Mao Zedong, the interior's share of industrial output actually rose, as growing tensions with the Soviet Union created **geopolitical** advantages from strengthening the western provinces. The economic policies introduced by Mao's successor, Deng Xiaoping, soon put an end to the relatively high level of equality enjoyed by China's citizens and regions.

China's GDP per capita, at $10,276 in December 2019, disguises considerable regional variations that exist today. 40% of China's population currently live in rural areas, with the remaining 60% living in urban areas. These urban areas are not evenly distributed, but are disproportionately situated in the coastal provinces. The mean urban income in China is more than twice the mean rural income.

The government's 'open-door' policy towards foreign direct investment (FDI) meant that, throughout the 1980s, investors from British-controlled Hong Kong and Japan became involved in manufacturing within China, particularly in the Pearl River Delta (PRD) region of Guangdong province. Provinces were given the freedom to pursue the comparative and **initial advantages** they enjoyed (coastal provinces enjoyed the most due to their location favouring trade) and China was simultaneously starting to become integrated into the world economy.

Development of China's Core - SEZs and Growth Poles from the 1980s:

To ensure this development strategy brought the required flow of capital, Deng Xiaoping authorised the creation of China's first wave of SEZs from 1980. Shenzhen, Zhuhai and Shantou (Guangdong province) and Xiamen (Fujian province) became SEZs, with the government offering investors cheap land, tax incentives and high-quality infrastructure. Shenzhen's growth has been the most spectacular, with its population climbing from 30,000 in the late-1970s to 175,000 in 1985 and more than 12 million by 2017.

Shenzhen has been transformed from a city of sweatshops to the home of global tech companies, such as Huawei and Tencent. (Image: ID 88199262 © Yongnian Gui | Dreamstime.com)

Through the 1980s and 1990s, more 'open cities' (SEZs and ETDZs) were set up in China's coastal areas, to help maintain the rapid inflow of FDI, and further develop the market economy in these areas. The ETDZs included Tianjin, Guangzhou, Zhanjiang and the Minhang District of Shanghai. The Pudong New Area of Shanghai also gained special economic status in 1993, enjoying similar openness as the other SEZs but with additional preferential policies. The increasing number of SEZs and ETDZs helped with the process of mobilising China's huge army of workers for industrial-based employment, as well as encouraging the exploitation of the country's vast mineral reserves.

China's development strategy was heavily biased towards the eastern provinces. The approach followed the 'ladder step' doctrine, whereby each region represented a step on the development ladder.

The coast, on a higher step, had a comparative advantage over inland areas, because of its existing infrastructure, and access to Pacific trade routes, so it was easier for the coast to be modernised first. The aim was to make the coastal areas globally-competitive, so they would be attractive to foreign investment. The new industrial sites established in the south-east coastal region, such as in Shenzhen and Zhuhai (within the now larger Pearl River Delta Economic Zone in Guangdong province) were to act as **growth poles** for the surrounding areas. Their role was to advance the technology transformation in China, from traditional and often high-energy consuming industries, to higher value-added consumer industries. Guangdong could boast 171,000 foreign funded enterprises in 2018.

The SEZs were based on the ideas of the **core-periphery model**, with the hope that as the SEZs developed, the wealth generated by the east coast core area would 'trickle down' to the inland, peripheral areas through positive **spread effects**, creating regional convergence. However, the downside was the likelihood that the special privileges afforded to the coastal areas, as well as the **multiplier effect** arising from **cumulative causation**, would discourage foreign investment in the interior, and so increase the wealth gap within China. Another impact of the SEZs was the pull they had for labourers in the countryside who knew that a job in an SEZ would provide a higher, and more regular, income than from farming. This invariably led to negative **backwash effects**, creating regional divergence. The relative unattractiveness of inland China can be seen by Tibet having only 266 foreign enterprises in 2018.

China's Core Region in Focus:

China's core region exists along the east coast, containing three major global hubs centred on Beijing/Tianjin, Shanghai and Guangdong province. The core region is responsible for most of the wealth-building economic activity and investment. Its three global hubs account for 21% of China's population and about 40% of its GDP. In addition, there are various sub-core areas in the coastal strip between the main global hubs. In fact, China has at least 160 cities with a population of more than a million, and most are located in the coastal provinces. The wealthiest economies in the core are the coastal municipalities of Beijing, Tianjin and Shanghai, with GDP per person figures in 2018 exceeding $18,000. Beijing occupied top spot with a figure of $21,269. The coastal provinces of Jiangsu, Zhejiang, Fujian, Guangdong and Shandong all enjoyed GDP per person figures in excess of $11,500.

Beijing's importance is linked to its capital city role. In addition, it is China's largest software production centre, and home to the Zhongguancun technology hub which is widely regarded as China's 'Silicon Valley'. The city has been transformed from an industrial to a service-based economy. Shanghai is China's commercial and financial centre, as well as a major industrial and trading city. It is the country's main gateway to the rest of the world through its huge port complex. Guangdong province, including nearby Hong Kong, contains a huge variety of industrial enterprises. At the heart of the province is the PRD Economic Zone, now being morphed into the even larger 'Greater Bay Area'. It has attracted a substantial amount of overseas investment from companies manufacturing electronics, domestic appliances, toys, clothing and footwear. Its population grew by more than one-third between 2000 and 2010.

China's Periphery Region in Focus:

China's periphery is to be found in the central and western parts of the country, and is best exemplified by the provinces of Xinjiang, Tibet, Qinghai, Yunnan, Guizhou, Gansu and Sichuan, all of which have GDP per person figures below $7,500. The periphery significantly lags behind China's coastal core region in terms of economic activity, investment and discretionary spending by consumers.

The central regions mainly concentrate on energy production, the extraction of raw materials, machinery manufacturing, and other heavy or lower value-added forms of manufacturing, while the western regions tend to focus on agriculture, forestry, raw materials and industries for local markets.

However, parts of the periphery have benefited from being resource frontiers, resulting in the development of secondary core areas. Chongqing municipality, in the upstream Yangtze River basin, is an example of a highly urbanised and industrialised city region in the periphery. Over 8 million people live in Chongqing itself, and around 32 million people are living in the wider urban region. Its GDP per person figure is just under $10,000, a factor in attracting half a million migrant workers from the surrounding provinces each year. Investment-driven manufacturing, particularly of automobiles and electronics, has boosted the wealth of the area, with much of this coming from Chinese companies rather than overseas firms.

Chongqing is also China's largest inland port, and a key city in the **Great Western Development Strategy** ('Open Up the West Initiative') launched in 2000, acting as a growth pole for the interior. Its proximity to the Three Gorges Dam, providing cheap electricity and reliable water supplies has provided industry with advantageous access to these key resources. The Three Gorges Dam project on the Yangtze River in Hubei province, has therefore become a pivotal part of China's development drive to open up the interior and spread the benefits of economic growth, including more FDI, to more peripheral areas, thereby extending the wealth of the core further inland.

Elsewhere in the periphery, state-owned industries and subsistence farming remain central aspects of the economy. Communications are generally limited. Inequality is also very marked between different rural areas of the periphery. For example, the fertile floodplains of the Yangtze valley provide farmers with more lucrative cash crops than the salty and sandy plain of the north, or the mountainous west. The poorest provinces in the periphery are Guizhou, Gansu and Yunnan, with GDP per person figures in 2018 below $6,500. Gansu occupied bottom spot with a figure of just $4,725.

Under the 'ladder step' doctrine, the periphery is expected to eventually catch up with the development and wealth levels of the core, but this depends on whether the spread effects from the core will ever outweigh the backwash effects. In addition, not all coastal or near-coastal provinces have reaped the rewards of China's economic drive. This is witnessed in the decaying industrial heartland of China's north-east, where massive state-financed industrial zones still rule.

GDP per capita for each of China' provinces, municipalities and regions in 2018, measured in US$. China's average GDP per capita of $9,770 in 2018 ($10,276 in 2019) masks the huge inequality in wealth between China's east coast core region and much of the peripheral interior. (Source: National Bureau of Statistics, China)

Economic Challenges Facing China's North-East:

The north-east region, encompassing the provinces of Liaoning, Jilin and Heilongjiang, has fallen on hard times in the past two decades. As China's east and south have got rich, in the rush to a market economy, China's north-east has been left behind. The region produced 16% of China's industrial output in the early 1980s, despite containing just 8% of the population. Cars, steel, ships and oil brought wealth to the area. However, by the beginning of the 21st century industrial output was down to 9%, as the frenzied economic growth moved to Shanghai and the southern province of Guangdong. The north-east has become China's 'Rust Belt', with provincial GDP per person figures between $6,500 and $9,000, providing the government with a severe challenge to turnaround.

In 2003, the government announced its 'Revitalize Northeast China' regional development policy. The aim was to rejuvenate the region's traditional industry through financial support and economic reforms. State-owned factories, which dominated production during the communist years, have been slowly released from inflexible government control, and expected to compete in the marketplace, and produce economic returns. While some have thrived, many others have struggled. What is uncertain, is how many inefficient factories still exist today, and the level of cash flow required from China's banks to prop them up.

Therefore, China's intractable problem is how to deal with the thousands of obsolete state-run factories in the region, in order to avoid the fallout from the growing level of unemployment and poverty, as well as the repercussions of environmental disasters. So far, there has been $8 billion of government spending, in a renewed attempt to rehabilitate the north-east region. The focus has been on closing, or privatising, the inefficient state-owned factories, while workers are being retrained for more modern assembly-line production or even software engineering.

The real test for regeneration will be whether foreign investment, from the likes of Japan and South Korea, can be attracted to the north-east. Dalian is the only city in the region with global ambitions that might be achievable in the near future. It is trying to surpass Bangalore, India, as the world's capital for **technology outsourcing**, and the rapid expansion of its software industry suggests it has a chance. The city has attracted foreign investment from US companies, such as Dell, Hewlett-Packard and IBM, although by far the biggest source of investment has come from Japan. Yet, despite the positive signs from Dalian, it remains to be seen whether the rest of the region as a whole can regain its former glory. High *unemployment and a reputation for corruption hamper the modernisation of the north-east.*

Recent Attempts to Reduce Regional Inequality:

China has been building close to 4,000km of railway tracks annually, with 80% being in China's central and western regions, areas where poverty remains an intractable problem for the government. The majority of new rail lines are high-speed rail tracks capable of supporting China's bullet trains (designed and manufactured in the country) that operate at up to 350 km/h. New roads and railways are helping farmers and rural businesses to sell in larger markets.

Although Yunnan province ranks as one of China's poorest regions, with GDP per person below $6,000, the 'trickle down' effects from economic growth in China's core are gradually being felt. (Image: © Alan Chapple)

Since 2016, an anti-poverty campaign by President Xi has started to tackle the problem of rural poverty by relocating households from remote or challenging rural locations to government-subsidised homes in more hospitable locations, either nearby or some distance away. In Guizhou province, around 750,000 people were moved to new villages and towns during 2017. The government hopes that similar resettlement schemes across rural China will remove 30 million people from extreme poverty by 2020, almost ending the existence of extreme poverty in China.

In the Tibet Autonomous Region (where 90% of the population is ethnic Tibetan), as well as in the Xinjiang-Uighur Autonomous Region (46% ethnic Uighur), government regional policy since 2000 has included the Great Western Development Strategy (bringing new infrastructure such as transport, HEP plants, energy, and telecommunications), advertising campaigns to attract foreign investment, and an increased focus on environmental protection (such as afforestation schemes).

Although the Tibet Autonomous Region remains one of China's poorest, with its GDP per person figure below $6,000, it has enjoyed the largest reductions in extreme poverty since 2010. Between 2010 and 2013 poverty here fell from 34% of its population to 19%. In January 2019, the regional government claimed that 180,000 had been lifted out of poverty during 2018 alone, and predicts an end to extreme poverty in the region by the end of 2019.

Despite the improvement in living standards in Tibet and Xinjiang, many locals view the motives of the government with suspicion. Simultaneous to the investment through the Great Western Development Strategy, there has been a deliberate government policy to encourage the in-migration of ethnic Han Chinese to these provinces. Tibetans and Uighurs worry that this large-scale population resettlement is part of a state-led plan to dilute their own ethnic cultures, as well as weakening local support for independence from China.

Waves of mass migration from China's heartland have increased Xinjiang's Han population from 6% in 1949 to around 40% today. The Uighur Muslim minority in Xinjiang have also had to contend with the government's 're-education camps', a system of internment camps to tackle extremism. Critics claim that these high-security prison camps have been built for the systematic brainwashing of hundreds of thousands of Uighurs.

Repression in the Xinjiang-Uighur Autonomous Region:

In the western region of Xinjiang, campaigns have been launched by China's government against the culture and religion of the Uighur people. There are more than 10 million Uighurs in Xinjiang, forming the largest Turkic speaking and Muslim minority ethnic group in the region. The campaigns against the Uighurs have been justified on the grounds of national security, particularly the need to combat terrorism and religious extremism. It is believed that hundreds of Uighurs travelled to Syria to fight with Islamic State (IS) and other militant groups.

Ürümqi is the capital of the Xinjiang-Uighur Autonomous Region. Situated near the northern route of the Silk Road, it has a population today of around 3 million. (Image: ID 138848869 © Aleksandar Pavlovic | Dreamstime.com)

Since 2014, members of the Uighurs (and some other Muslim ethnic minorities) have been detained, for weeks, months or even longer periods, in newly built 're-education camps', with UN-backed reports suggesting as many as 1 million Uighurs have been forced into detention. It appears that the majority have been taken to these camps without trial or any charges brought against them. Observation towers, razor wire and sophisticated surveillance systems feature alongside the camps' classrooms and dormitories.

The camps are aimed at changing the religious beliefs, political ideologies and language of the Uighur people. The Chinese government has denied their existence as internment camps, describing them as 'vocational education centres' where 'trainees' attend voluntarily to learn Mandarin and gain job skills. Yet, former inmates have claimed they were imprisoned for merely following Islamic traditions, such as wearing long beards.

Other reports suggest that the detention of whole extended families has led to young children being placed in state orphanages. Further actions taken against the Uighur minority have included the closure of mosques, men forbidden to grow beards, and women forced to remove head coverings. In addition, a state-sponsored 'cultural exchange' initiative has seen more than one million local government officials deployed to spend time in the homes of Uighur families. The government calls it the 'Pair Up and Become Family' campaign. Critics see it as a way of extending surveillance to within the home. Everyday life for Uighurs is also affected by high-level security in the province's main streets, including the widespread use of facial-recognition CCTV cameras and thousands of checkpoints for pedestrians and vehicles.

The region's mineral wealth, especially from oil and gas, and its SEZ status have brought considerable investment into Xinjiang. However, the in-migration of Han Chinese and the uneven spoils from the region's economic growth have created simmering ethnic tensions, despite the rise in living standards enjoyed by nearly all its residents. The Chinese government boasts about the absence of terrorist attacks in recent years, claiming the region now enjoys social stability and unity. Whether the policy of internment reduces or amplifies the resentment of the Uighurs in the long-term remains to be seen.

Poverty, Inequality and a Two-Speed Economy:

The need to tackle poverty in China's rural areas is a priority, since only India has more poor people than China. Although more than 400 million people have been lifted out of extreme poverty in the last two decades, there were still thought to be 175 million living below the World Bank's $1.90 dollars a day benchmark for extreme poverty in 2010. Official government figures suggest that 45 million were living below the national poverty line at the end of 2016. The government hopes that 30 million of these people will no longer experience extreme poverty by 2020. In the richest provinces, extreme poverty had almost entirely been eliminated by the end of 2019 if government sources are to be believed. Local officials in Jiangsu province claimed that just 17 people from 6 households were living below its benchmark of 6,000 yuan ($863) a year due to a successful campaign that had helped lift 2.54 million people out of extreme poverty in the past four years.

Despite the reduction in extreme poverty, moderate poverty remains a reality of life for the majority of China's rural citizens. Notwithstanding government policies to raise the price of agricultural products, and reduce the tax burden for farmers, the 650 million people living in the countryside are still relatively poor and uneducated, although new roads and railways are helping local businesses to reach out to larger markets.

China's economic development has also created social problems. The economic reforms have favoured the coastal provinces, whose booming economies contrast with large parts of the interior where state-owned enterprises are still the norm, and have difficulty remaining competitive. The huge flood of migrant labour from the interior to the coast, estimated to involve 170 million of China's 290 million migrants, has changed the demography of the countryside.

Geographically (inland v coastal), sector-wise (primary v secondary) and ownership (state-run v private), China demonstrates the characteristics of a two-speed economy. Even in the cities, poverty can be found within one or two blocks of the more upmarket residential or business areas. Many people are engaged in informal work, especially near tourist locations, and others resort to begging.

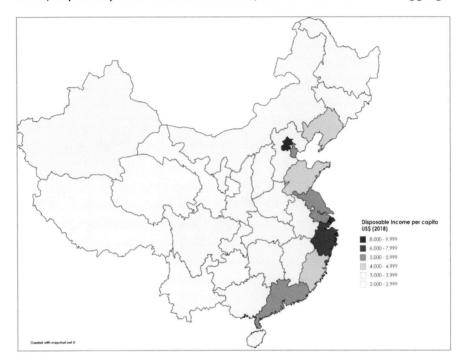

Disposable income per capita for China' provinces, municipalities and regions in 2018 shows the higher living standards enjoyed by the population in the east coast core region. The mean income for households in Shanghai and Beijing was in excess of $8,000. The mean income in Qinghai, Yunnan, Guizhou, Gansu and Tibet was below $3,000. (Source: National Bureau of Statistics, China)

Despite the relative poverty evident in China's cities, life in the countryside remains worse for the vast majority. In all of China's provinces, the gap between urban and rural incomes is huge. Urban households in the Shanghai municipality enjoyed a mean income of $9,525 in 2018 (the highest in China), dwarfing the mean income of $4,252 for rural households in the same municipality. At the same time, the mean income of urban households in Gansu province was only $4,194 (the lowest in China), yet this was still far higher than the mean income of just $1,233 for rural households in the same province. For China's government, urbanisation must continue if the country is to escape the **middle-income trap**.

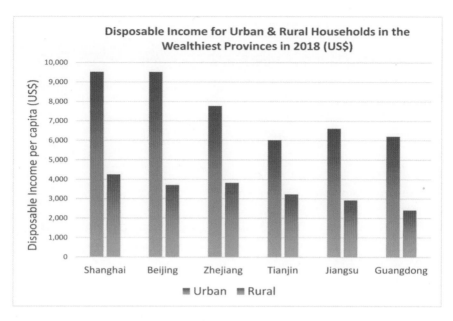

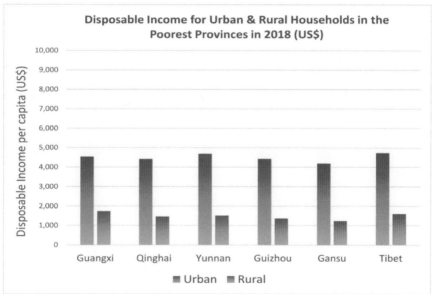

The income gap between urban and rural households is high throughout China, with urban residents at least twice as well off. Shanghai residents have the highest incomes; Gansu residents the lowest. (Source: National Bureau of Statistics, China)

Evaluation of Regional Policy:

Coastal cities continue to have a clear comparative advantage for most manufacturing industries over inland areas, despite rising costs of production, such as labour costs. For e-commerce and service industries, the coast offers huge advantages linked to market size. The effects of foreign investment and export-led growth have been to increase wealth levels considerably in these coastal locations, with the outcome that economic and social inequalities between core and peripheral regions in China have widened over time.

China's Gini index stood at 0.468 in 2018, having peaked at 0.491 in 2008. Such a score (0 = total equality; 1 = total inequality) shows that the gap in income distribution is still relatively large. China has lost its status of being one of the most equal places in the world, and now ranks as one of the most unequal. The richest 1% of the population hold one-third of household wealth, with research by Forbes and Credit Suisse identifying 476 billionaires and 4.4 million millionaires in 2019.

Communications and transport remain limited in much of the interior, although recent government investment is beginning to address the problems. Yet, far more workers in the periphery are still tied to the low wages of obsolete and inefficient state-run industries, many of which are viewed as 'zombie' companies due to their failure to bring economic returns.

The urban-rural divide in China is stark, with per person income in the countryside being less than one-third of the cities. The role of the state exacerbated this inequality, by gifting many urban residents their homes during the privatisation wave of the 1990s. Simultaneously, young rural-urban migrants have suffered discrimination due to the Hukou household registration system of residency permits. Rural-registered workers in cities don't enjoy the social security, healthcare and education benefits that are offered to their urban equivalents, and they regularly suffer wage discrimination at the hands of unscrupulous employers. This limits the spoils of economic development available to the rural poor.

The outcome of the growing economic disparities has been unrest, with protests over income inequality, land rights and local corruption taking place. Uneven economic growth has led to growing resentment by the people living in the underdeveloped inland regions, who perceive that other regions, particularly the coastal ones, are prospering at their expense.

Difficulties Judging the Effectiveness of Regional Policy:

China is a vast country with an equally huge population. The scale of the problem (regional disparities) is large compared to the financial resources of the government (whose relatively high debt must be managed carefully to ensure sustainability).

Although the Communist Party has maintained its power for decades, regional development policy changes frequently (each 5-year plan has addressed the regional development issue in different ways).

Regional disparities could well have been far greater in the absence of regional policy (it's impossible to know what the regional disparities would have been like without any government action.

The topic is highly political, and censorship is very evident in China, so much of the information on regional policy (from journals, articles, news reports) could be biased.

Investment comes from both the public sector and the private sector, and one can't be sure if private sector investment is due to the government's regional development policy or not (therefore, should the government take all, or just some of, the credit?).

So far, the rate of urbanisation in China (around 2-3% a year) has been slower than the rate of China's economic growth (6-10% a year). It is likely that the government will want to pursue faster urban expansion over the coming decades, in order to achieve its ambitious plans for economic improvement. About 220 million rural labourers moved to the cities looking for work between 1979 and 2014, and it is likely that another 100 million will have moved by 2020. The risk of greater unrest from the 600 million or so remaining rural residents is a fear of the government.

Rural land-grabbing close to the cities has also been a problem. The construction of new roads, factories and residential areas has led to the eviction of rural households, with very little compensation paid. Over 60,000 square kilometres of farmland have been lost in the last two decades.

The government has tried to tackle some of the problems of the periphery by improving the infrastructure of the interior, in order to attract more prospective investors. Measures include the Three Gorges Dam project, subsidies for businesses moving to inland cities, such as Chongqing, a new train line from Beijing to Tibet, and allowing exceptions to the 'one-child' policy (well before the policy was scrapped in 2016). However, the trickle-down effects to the countryside have been slow. For most young rural adults, the only way to better their lives has been to migrate to the cities. Remittances sent back by these migrants to their family members in the interior do help to reduce the wealth gap, but the overall consequences of migration have led to an increasingly ageing rural population, with too few entrepreneurial and creative people to kickstart the rural economies.

Regional Development and Inequality in China Concluded:

It would appear, overall, that China's attempt to develop its western regions has had varying effects on the economic development of the interior. While massive investment has boosted the output of the interior, effectively raising the GDP in all western regions, the Great Western Development Strategy has failed to achieve its goal of eliminating the economic gap between China's eastern and western provinces. Much of the GDP growth enjoyed by inland provinces has been achieved by state-backed energy and infrastructure projects, rather than private sector investment in manufacturing. It remains to be seen whether the interior becomes a more attractive location for investment in the future as costs of production and other **diseconomies** increase in the core.

Quick Questions:

- *Why has government investment focused much more on the coastal provinces, rather than the inland provinces?*
- *What are the main roles of the inland provinces?*
- *Where can China's three major global hubs be found?*
- *What are the key differences between these global hubs?*
- *How is China's periphery expected to benefit from the economic growth generated by the core region?*
- *What are the benefits of the Three Gorges Dam project?*
- *Which province has the lowest per person GDP?*
- *Why do wealth levels vary between different rural areas in China?*
- *How has the Chinese government tried to address the problem of poverty in the rural areas?*
- *What factors have contributed to poverty in China's urban areas?*
- *What are the challenges facing China's North-East?*
- *How is the Chinese government trying to help the North-East?*
- *Why is development a 'mixed blessing' for regions such as Tibet and Xinjiang?*
- *What has happened to income distribution in China over time?*
- *What evidence suggests that the gap between China's core and periphery is increasing rather than decreasing?*

Tasks & Discussion:

- *Why has China's east coast developed into the country's core region?*
- *To what extent have the backwash effects associated with the development of China's core region exceeded the spread effects?*
- *Outline the major challenges facing the development of China's periphery.*
- *Explain the rise and fall of China's North-East.*
- *Discuss the positive and negative consequences of rural-urban migration in China.*
- *Outline the social and economic problems that China's rapid economic growth has created within the country.*
- *To what extent has the Great Western Development Strategy achieved its objectives?*

Chapter 3: The Economic Challenges Facing China

For China's citizens, economic growth has brought about rising living standards, but the coastal provinces have enjoyed far more of the riches than the interior. As a result, China's economic path has been at odds with the communist ideology of economic equality. The country has been successful in lifting 400 million of its people out of extreme poverty, yet rural poverty and regional inequality remain ever-present threats to the country's stability. China's entry into the global economy, linked to its membership of the WTO and its abundant supply of cheap labour, helped to transform global supply chains and fuelled a period of hyper-globalisation from the 1990s.

However, replicating the impressive growth rates of the past two decades will be a considerable challenge for China's leaders. Rising wages have already eroded the 'cheap China' manufacturing model for TNCs. An ongoing trade war with the US, involving tariffs and technology tensions, has further reduced the appeal of China as the 'workshop to the world'. The need to transition its economy from low-value manufacturing to high-tech products and services, as well as increasing domestic consumption is recognised by the government. As a result, President Xi has promised to deliver high-quality growth over high-speed development in the coming decades.

Investment, Over-Expansion, Debt and Sustainability:

China's massive trade imbalance with the US and EU, resulting from the explosive growth of the past few decades, has helped create huge **foreign exchange reserves**, and this spare money has had significant repercussions. Although its trade surplus should be largely beneficial for China, much of the excess capital has been re-invested in residential, commercial and industrial facilities. The downside of this over-expansion is the potential danger of it creating an overheated economy. Inflation has been rising, and is higher than in the advanced economies. The government has looked to impose a ceiling on wage rises in some provinces, and put in price controls on foodstuffs and commodities; however, these measures have not been overly successful.

Therefore, despite the success of China's economy, there are still concerns about its **sustainability**. The economy is unbalanced, and so the risk of a calamitous crash is considerable. Foreign companies, operating in China, often fail to understand the domestic market, leading to nearly half failing within two years. The government's spending on infrastructure and business growth has been relentless, and investment levels for many years have been at an unprecedented 40-50% of the country's GDP. The danger is that much of the spending will never generate an economic return, meaning losses for the investors and lenders. The credit boom in China has led to the country's total debts doubling relative to total GDP, from 125% of GDP in 2008 to 250% of GDP by 2016. Government debt, in 2017, was a more manageable 47% of China's GDP.

A large quantity of these debts is currently hidden by financial institutions, operating as 'shadow' banks, through their informal lending to businesses. The biggest single group of debtors are state-owned enterprises, of which China has around 150,000. Many of these are viewed as 'zombie' companies in that they are not financially viable and operate in sectors where there is excess capacity. Up until now, government policy has been to rescue any state-run enterprises or local private companies experiencing financial difficulties, but with the debts of some companies escalating this is no longer sustainable. Business failures will have to be allowed, even though this could impact on investor confidence in China. One advantage for China is that it is less dependent on borrowing from abroad than many other emerging economies, so is less susceptible to a sudden loss of confidence among foreign lenders precipitating a financial crisis in the country.

Ordinary Chinese citizens still tend to save, rather than spend much of their disposable income, and although this provides the banks with money for business lending, it also means that domestic consumer demand is lower than in many other economies. Household consumption was just 36% of GDP in 2010. The domestic property market was particularly weak during 2014, with the glut of newly built housing resulting in price falls. Factory output slowed to its lowest level since the Global Financial Crisis, with the result that GDP growth fell to 7.3%, the lowest level since 1991. Urban property prices have since risen sharply, but this brings with it the risk of higher consumer debt levels. To make matters worse, there has been increasing scepticism about the reliability of China's economic data. China's GDP was officially valued at $13.60 trillion for 2018 (and more than $14 trillion for 2019), but some analysts believe that the country has been overstating the size of its economy by almost 10% ($1 trillion), with corrupt provincial officials to blame for providing bogus economic data.

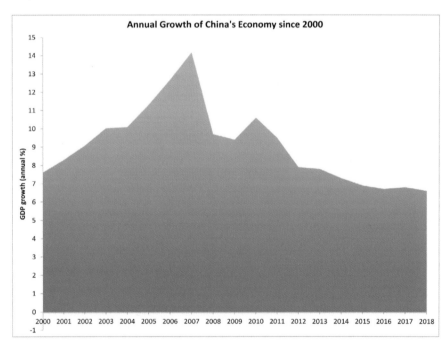

Annual % change in the GDP of China since 2000, measured in US$. Growth was rapid until the Global Financial Crisis, but a slowdown is now occurring. GDP growth in 2019 was just 6.1%. (Source: World Bank Data)

Economic Reforms and More Sustainable Growth:

China's leader, Xi Jinping, has tried to crack down on corruption. His government has announced economic reforms to control the amount of investment and spending. In February 2014, China's central bank, The People's Bank of China, removed nearly $8 billion from the money markets, to control the amount of credit in the country's financial system. Unsurprisingly, the government's GDP growth target for 2015 was lowered to 7%, on the basis that China is entering a stage of medium-high growth, known as the "new normal". Official figures indicate the economy grew by 6.9% in 2015, 6.7% in 2016, 6.9% in 2017 and 6.6% in 2018. Growth during 2019, at just 6.1%, was the slowest since 1990, a sign of the slower but more sustainable high-quality growth that the government is seeking to achieve.

Xi Jinping (centre), President of China since 2013, with the other BRICS leaders - Michel Temer, Narendra Modi, Vladimir Putin and Jacob Zuma - at a meeting held in Hangzhou, China in 2016. (Image: © Government ZA, CC)

However, China's attempt to engineer its economy away from exports, and towards services and domestic consumption, has already unsettled the markets. Such a policy takes time, and there is no guarantee of success. The first nine months of 2015 saw a series of interest rate cuts to boost economic growth, but weak factory output figures, and a surprise devaluation of the yuan in August, led to increased fears of a Chinese-led global slowdown. 24th August 2015 became China's 'Black Monday' with its stock markets experiencing dramatic losses as a mood of panic among investors dominated share trading. The Shanghai Composite index, the main benchmark in China, registered an 8.5% slump on the 24th, its biggest fall since 2007.

In 2018, there was further gloom for investors as the Shanghai Composite index fell by more than 25%, making it one of the world's worst performing stock markets. The knock-on effects extended to the health of the global economy, as China accounts for around one-third of global GDP growth, and its industry is closely integrated into international supply chains.

China's desperate attempts to stabilise its stock markets are not its only concern. Some reports suggest that the government may have to make up to six million state workers redundant over the next few years, as the economy shifts from manufacturing to services. Tertiary sector growth was around 7% in 2019, while secondary sector growth was below 6%. At present, each 1% of GDP growth has the potential to create nearly 2 million new jobs, and current growth should keep unemployment below 5%. Whether the population accept the repercussions on jobs and living standards in the longer term remains to be seen. The possibility of protest and unrest looms, particularly if GDP growth plunges below 6%.

'China fears falling into the "middle-income country trap" where nations, like many in Latin America, never make it to the top tier of the world's richest countries.' (Linda Yueh, The Times Newspaper 27.08.15)

youth unemployment
18-25 → 25%.

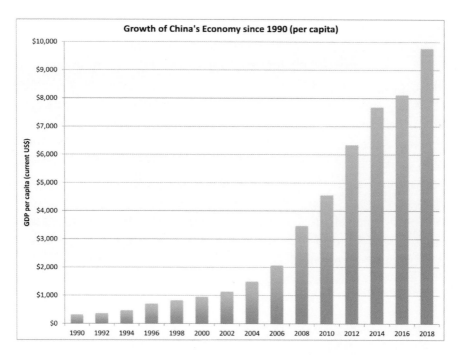

Growth of GDP per capita in China since 1990, measured in US$. China's GDP per capita reached $10,276 in December 2019. Incomes have risen for people throughout China, but the greatest rise has been in the coastal cities. (Source: World Bank Data)

High-tech Industries, Innovation and Chinese Global Brands:

The future for much of China is likely to involve a shift to more high-tech industries, particularly in the coastal provinces where the workforce is acquiring more skills, allowing the country to move up the value chain. In fact, the country's attempts to create a **knowledge-based economy** will be vital in delivering a higher standard of living for most of its people, and achieving the status of an HIC. China's education system is certainly playing its part in the country's increasing economic fortune. Nine years of compulsory education is provided free of charge, benefiting 160 million students. As a result, the literacy rate is above 90%, and more than 20% of students go on to higher education. More than 8 million students graduated in 2019, but the white-collar jobs which they desire are still in short supply.

Research and development involving medical technology is also likely to be a key area for China, given the rapid ageing of its population. Meanwhile, the benefit of its continued investment in national infrastructure projects will be to open up more of the interior, where costs are lower, to attract industries looking for low and semi-skilled labour. However, China needs to encourage an even more vibrant private sector, as the unfair competition from state-owned companies is still a shackle on the economy. This includes preferential access to bank loans, and exclusive control of industries such as finance, heavy engineering and energy. Therefore, despite the economic reforms of recent decades, state-owned enterprises still account for one-third of China's GDP and around two-thirds of its outbound investment.

Global Rank	Company	Sector	HQ	Revenue (US $ billions)
2	State Grid	Energy	Beijing	349
3	Sinopec	Energy	Beijing	327
4	China National Petroleum	Energy	Beijing	326
23	China State Construction Engineering (CSCEC)	Engineering & Construction	Beijing	156
26	Industrial & Commercial Bank of China (ICBC)	Banking	Beijing	153
29	Ping An Insurance	Insurance	Shenzhen	144
31	China Construction Bank	Banking	Beijing	139
36	SAIC Motor	Automobiles	Shanghai	129
40	Agricultural Bank of China	Banking	Beijing	122
42	China Life Insurance	Insurance	Beijing	120
46	Bank of China	Banking	Beijing	115
53	China Mobile Communications	Telecommunications	Beijing	110
56	China Railway Engineering	Engineering & Construction	Beijing	103
58	China Railway Construction	Engineering & Construction	Beijing	101
65	Dongfeng Motor	Automobiles	Wuhan	93
72	Huawei Investment & Holding	Telecommunications	Shenzhen	89
86	China Resources	Pharmaceuticals	Hong Kong	82
87	China National Offshore Oil	Energy	Beijing	81
91	China Communications Construction	Engineering & Construction	Beijing	79
96	Pacific Construction Group	Engineering & Construction	Ürümqi	77
98	Sinochem Group	Chemicals & Energy	Beijing	77

Chinese companies ranking in the top 100 globally (Source: Data from Fortune Global 500 for 2018)

China is trying to develop its home-grown industries and show more innovation. Although more than half the world's electronic devices, such as mobile phones, are assembled in China, the ubiquitous 'made in China' labels disguise the fact that China's assembly lines are often manufacturing products whose designs and key components originate from other countries. So, despite playing a major role in the hyper-globalisation of supply chains, it has benefited less from its involvement in global **value chains**. Currently, China has few truly **global brands**, despite having 21 companies ranking in the top 100 of the Fortune Global 500 listing for 2018. Its largest companies are mainly state-owned rather than private, with the top ones involved in energy, such as Sinopec Group, China National Petroleum (PetroChina) and State Grid.

China's 13th Five-Year Plan (2016-2020) focused on moving away from low-value manufacturing to higher value products and services. A key component is the '**Made in China 2025**' plan to obtain a bigger share of global production chains and reach the next level of development. Under the initiative, the Chinese government wants the country to become a global leader in ten key industries, including information technology, robotics, green energy, aerospace equipment, medicine and medical devices. It is this plan to dominate certain strategic sectors that has stirred fear abroad, despite much of China's current technology lagging behind the global leading edge.

The success of its car industry is a sign that China is capable of moving into new manufacturing areas, and competing successfully with the foreign competition. China is the world's leading car manufacturer, and although US, Japanese and European companies have plants in China, the real achievements are from its own homegrown companies, such as the state-owned corporations, Dongfeng, SAIC and Chery, or the private automaker, Geely.

These companies have been making their own cars since the 1990s, initially showing a close resemblance to models from rival manufacturers. However, in recent years they have been developing new concept cars, and bringing out new models, suggesting that bringing innovative designs and features to the market are within the capabilities of Chinese companies. They have established an increasing number of joint venture operations with European and American manufacturers, and also have ambitious plans to extend their influence abroad. Dongfeng agreed a joint venture with Renault in late 2013, and in early 2014 it secured a 14% stake in the struggling French carmaker, PSA Peugeot Citroen, by agreeing to invest €800 million in the company. Meanwhile, Chery and Jaguar Land Rover opened a new plant at Changsu in late-2014, in a joint venture operation involving nearly $2 billion of investment.

China's Copycat Firms:

Chinese firms have been accused of copying the designs of Western companies.

James Dyson, the inventor of the bagless vacuum cleaner, has attacked Chinese companies for stealing the intellectual property rights to his company's products, especially the bladeless Air Multiplier fan. Dyson is spending £2 million each year to protect the patents that his company owns from at least 10 Chinese firms who are manufacturing a near-identical fan. Dyson has also accused some of these firms of filing patents that are identical to his own patents.

In 2011, a number of fake, and unlicensed, Apple stores, similar in design and shopper experience to the official ones, were discovered in the south-western Chinese city of Kunming. They looked and felt so real that many of the employees thought they were working for Apple. Two were quickly shut down by Chinese officials for not having a proper licence, and a further 22 copycat Apple stores in the area were later uncovered.

Competing with China:

Companies manufacturing in HICs need to find new industries, or niche areas in existing industries, that gives them a competitive edge. Differentiating their products to emphasise their increased safety, reliability or quality over the outsourced products from China is one tactic that has been shown to work.

In the 'toxic toys' scandal, involving lead contamination of Mattel products made in China, American companies making toys in the US saw a huge jump in orders, as the public began to appreciate the importance of safety for their children, as well as recognise that high-quality, and often hand-crafted, toys from local manufacturers were worth the price premium.

The lesson for manufacturers is that there will always be a market for a domestic product that can stand out from the crowd of inferior goods from foreign competitors.

The Chinese government has made no secret of its desire to become self-sufficient in information technology. China is both the world's largest importer and consumer of semiconductors, yet currently manufactures just 16% of the chips that have fuelled its technology boom. Its 'Made in China 2025' plan aims to increase this figure to 70% by 2025.

But, even if China does manage to become a global powerhouse in high-tech sectors, such as semiconductors and robotics, further intractable challenges could yet jeopardise China's bid for superpower status. The emergence of other lower cost NICs in Africa and Asia will draw some TNCs away from China. Other TNCs may even move jobs back to their home country due to political or consumer pressure, a trend known as **reshoring**. Fortunately, China is perhaps better able than its rivals to manage its economic attractiveness, since its huge size and regional diversity ensure different economies exist within the one nation. The government hopes that any negative impact on investment arising from increased labour costs in the country's east coast core region will be balanced by firms moving to the interior to exploit the lower costs of production of China's periphery.

Furthermore, China is set to earn additional wealth from its own TNCs, which are likely to be major investors in the new economies of Africa and Asia. Chinese global telecommunications equipment brands, such as Huawei Technologies and ZTE Corporation, and the oil giant, PetroChina, will be more active abroad, although Huawei and ZTE have faced opposition from the US and several other foreign governments due to concerns over national security. Nevertheless, Huawei continues to play a key role in the upgrading of Vodafone's European and African mobile networks, having secured a major deal with Vodafone in early 2014.

US-China Trade War and Technology Tensions:

Throughout 2018 and 2019, tensions between the US and China on issues around trade and technology dominated the landscape of the global economy. A US investigation identified a range of discriminatory practices imposed by China's state-led economy, including unfair competition and restrictions on foreign ownership that necessitate the transfer of technology from US to Chinese companies, ultimately leading to intellectual property theft. In addition, China was accused of targeting US strategic industries with its own FDI, as well as conducting and supporting cyber-attacks abroad. US Trade Representative, Robert Lighthizer, claimed that China's unfair trade practices had cost the US at least $50 billion annually. Although China is the third-largest market for US exports, China enjoyed a $375 billion trade surplus with the US in 2017 (exporting $505 billion to the US while importing just $130 billion). The US wanted China to cut its trade surplus by $200 billion.

Initially, tariffs were imposed on imported washing machines and solar panels. In March 2018, Donald Trump signed further orders imposing a 25% tariff on imported steel and a 10% tariff on imported aluminium. China struck back with tariffs on US pork, wine, fruit and nuts. Both countries identified hundreds more products where tariffs of up to 25% would be imposed if the trade dispute wasn't resolved. By mid-2018, the US had imposed tariffs on $50 billion of Chinese goods, with China reacting similarly, imposing tariffs on many

American farm products. The US list was designed to hit products identified in the 'Made in China 2025' plan, such as semiconductors, industrial robots, electric vehicle motors, aircraft parts and cars. The inclusion of aircraft parts and cars indicated a pre-emptive strike by the US on China's attempt to dominate certain strategic sectors in the future, as none were exported to the US in 2017.

By September 2018, another round of tariffs marked a sharp escalation in the trade war. The US imposed tariffs on a further $200 billion worth of products from China, bringing the total to $250 billion of goods, accounting for approximately 45% of China's exports to the USA. The tariffs were initially levelled at 10%, but with a warning by the US that they would rise to 25% during 2019 if the dispute remained unresolved. China retaliated in a more restrained way, imposing tariffs on a further $60 billion of American goods, bringing the total to $110 billion. China promised to buy more agricultural, industrial and energy products from the US in an attempt to prevent a further round of tariffs during 2019. It also announced that it will allow foreign car makers to enjoy full ownership of car plants by 2022, rather than work with state-owned partners in joint venture operations, a move that addresses US concerns over the transfer of technology to potential competitors.

Nevertheless, China's trade surplus with the US increased to $419 billion in 2018 (exporting $539 billion while importing $120 billion). Despite extensive negotiations to resolve the trade dispute, in May 2019 Donald Trump announced an increase in tariffs from 10% to 25% on $200 billion of Chinese goods, hitting manufacturers of telecommunications equipment and computer circuit boards particularly hard. Similar tariffs on all remaining imports from China, estimated at around $325 billion, were threatened. China retaliated by imposing 25% tariffs on another $60 billion of US goods.

In August 2019, President Trump declared that 10% tariffs were to be applied to a further $300 billion of Chinese goods from September, with a threat to increase them to 25%, although the tariffs covering mobile phones, games consoles, computers, footwear and clothing were delayed until December. Subsequently, an additional tariff increase of 5% on imports from China was announced at the end of August in response to China's plans to impose further tariffs on $75 billion of US goods. Intense negotiations between the two sides to finally end the trade war led to the signing of an agreement aimed at easing the trade dispute in January 2020. As part of the deal, China pledged to boost US imports by $200 billion above 2017 levels, while the US agreed to halve some of the new tariffs it had imposed on China's exports. Nonetheless, both countries would continue to maintain the 25% tariff level on a significant proportion of each other's exports.

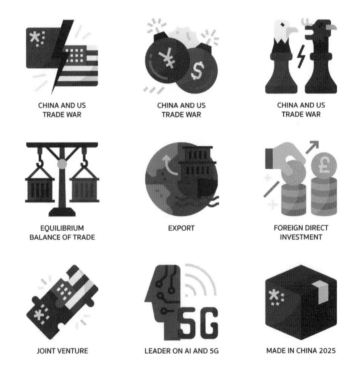

Implications of the US-China trade war. (Image ID 156282176 © Creativedoxfoto | Dreamstime.com)

The US-China trade war has inevitably led to a re-think among foreign TNCs, as well as large Chinese businesses, about the risks of their over-dependence on China as a manufacturing base. The imposition of punitive tariffs on Chinese exports to the US means there is an incentive to relocate production to countries not subject to such tariffs. Among the beneficiaries has been Vietnam which saw an upsurge in Chinese investment during 2019. Apple has reportedly asked its biggest suppliers, including Foxconn, to investigate the possibility of moving up to 30% of its supply chain out of China, with India and Vietnam the preferred destinations. However, relocation on this scale could take years to achieve given the diversity and sophistication of China's electronics manufacturing capacity.

Simultaneous to the on-going trade war between the US and China, both countries have been embroiled in arguments over the misuse of technology in matters of national security. Many of China's global high-tech leaders, such as Huawei and ZTE, while privately run, are believed to be supported and monitored by the government. Huawei was blocked by the US government from selling its latest smartphones through US carriers. The US also put in place measures to ban Huawei's telecommunications equipment from its broadband and mobile networks.

Technology tensions between the US and China reached new heights in May 2019 with the Trump administration adding Huawei to its 'entity list', a move which bans the company from acquiring technology from US firms without government approval. Almost immediately, Huawei's ability to use software or hardware from US companies, such as Google and Intel, was threatened.

Other countries have followed suit, citing concerns that Huawei's technology could be used by the Chinese government to gain backdoor access to sensitive information, including commercial secrets and national security affairs. The West's mistrust of China in the field of high-tech globalisation threatens the ambitions of its 'Made in China 2025' plan.

New Projects and Increasing Global Influence:

China's government, with $3.24 trillion of foreign exchange reserves available to spend at the end of 2017, has stepped up its investment in infrastructure projects that will enhance its regional connectivity.

It has already pledged to spend $150 billion annually to develop the 'Silk Road Economic Belt' and the '21st Century Maritime Silk Road'. These projects, together known as the '**Belt and Road Initiative**' (BRI) or 'One Belt One Road Initiative', aim to better connect its economy with Central Asia, the Middle East and Europe. The huge investment includes new ports, airports, roads, rail links and resource pipelines, with the possibility of creating a huge free trade zone and a 'belt of prosperity' through all the connected countries.

In addition, the establishment during 2015 of the Chinese-led Asian Infrastructure Investment Bank (AIIB) also promises to extend China's influence throughout Asia, while weakening that of the US. The AIIB is a multilateral lender with some 70 countries as members, alongside China, but without any US involvement. With China also heavily involved with the other BRICS economies in the New Development Bank (NDB), the days of the US as the sole superpower look numbered as China wields its economic muscle globally.

Employment, Energy and Population Challenges:

The strain of rapid urbanisation remains a major challenge. Industrialisation has had terrible consequences for urban environments, with China's cities being among the most polluted in the world. The provision of housing and services for the millions of migrants is also a substantial problem. In addition, China needs to find tens of millions of new urban jobs each year, in order to prevent the discontent that unemployment will bring.

China faces an inevitable long-term consequence from its thirty-five-year long enforcement of the 'one-child' policy. If current trends continue, its population will peak at 1.44 billion in 2029, before steadily declining. The repercussion of this is already happening, in the rapid ageing of its population. By 2050, 330 million Chinese (more than a quarter of the population) will be over 65. The negative change in China's dependency ratio will increase the costs of providing pensions, healthcare and appropriate housing, while reducing the availability of young, skilled and entrepreneurial workers. Tackling the economic and social consequences of its 'demographic time-bomb', resulting from a rapidly ageing population and a shrinking workforce, will not be straightforward for the Chinese leadership.

Keeping pace with the demand for energy is another challenge. Energy demand has doubled since 2000, and China's share of global energy demand is likely to reach 40% by 2030, from the current 18% level. China has been building up to 100 power stations a year recently, and will need to build a minimum of 40 new power stations every year for many years to come. The huge amounts of water used by power stations for cooling and driving steam turbine generators are contributing to acute water shortages too. More than half of China's cities, including Beijing, are desperately short of water, as is much of the far north.

Section of the Great Wall of China, north of Beijing. As many as 10 million tourists are attracted annually to the 21,000 km long fortification. However, some stretches of the UNESCO World Heritage site are badly affected by graffiti and vandalism. (Image: © Alan Chapple)

More positive is the country's potential for tourism which could provide an increasingly valuable source of revenue for China. Already, it accounts for around 11% of the economy, while employing almost 30 million people. Domestic tourism has been consistently strong due to China's rapidly growing number of middle-class citizens, with 10% annual growth experienced in the past decade. In addition, the 141 million overseas visitors to China in 2018 is evidence of China's global appeal. Numbers are expected to increase further once the global economy picks up following the devastating impacts on the tourism sector of the COVID-19 coronavirus pandemic during 2020. Tourist attractions and jobs have been supported by China's continuing investment in high-speed trains, airports and international-standard hotels.

Economic Impacts of the Coronavirus Outbreak

COVID-19, the disease caused by a new strain of coronavirus (SARS-CoV-2), spread rapidly from the city of Wuhan, Hubei province, during December 2019. The virus was reported to the World Health Organization (WHO) on 31st December.

A lack of action by the Chinese authorities was a feature of the early weeks of the outbreak. It wasn't until 23rd January 2020 that the Chinese government imposed a lockdown in Wuhan and other cities in Hubei to quarantine the population at the centre of the coronavirus outbreak. During February, restrictions were placed on people and businesses in many other parts of China. Wuhan's lockdown was lifted on 8th April, although restrictions on movement continued.

Between December 2019 and 10th April 2020, there were just over 83,000 confirmed cases of COVID-19 and 3,342 deaths according to official figures. 96% of the deaths were in Hubei province. The accuracy of the official figures was questioned, with initial testing focused only on patients with severe symptoms.

On 17th April, the authorities in Wuhan raised their official COVID-19 death toll by 1,290 to take into account deaths outside hospitals and new data from other sources. The latest figures brought the national death toll to 4,632.

China's economy was effectively idle during February 2020 due to the lockdowns and other restrictions that were rigorously enforced by its police and security forces. Manufacturing output fell far faster than during the 2007-2008 Global Financial Crisis. Services, including shops, restaurants, hotels, cinemas, transport and tourism, were also hugely impacted.

Factory output climbed in March with a gradual return to work being authorised by the government in many provinces, although quarantine rules continued to affect around one-third of China's 290 million migrant workers. Data released by the government showed the economy contracted by 6.8% between January and March 2020.

The outbreak was declared a global pandemic by the WHO on 11th March. As lockdowns and other isolation measures became more widespread across Europe, North America and other regions, much international business and trade came to a standstill and global stock markets crashed. For China, looking to kick-start its economy, the collapse in global demand for manufactured goods and services creates a greater challenge than the initial domestic lockdown.

Human Rights and Political Freedom:

One other significant issue has the potential to be a problem in the future; namely China's large-scale disregard for human rights and democracy. When government officials decide to build a new city, or construct a new airport, the people most affected are often not consulted. Cities go up, planes take-off, and the villages that were once there simply disappear. The displaced villagers may be compensated, but they are not allowed to stand in the way of progress. China's government makes decisions that balance the needs of all citizens over the long term. Mostly this has been successful, with sustained growth lifting hundreds of millions of people out of poverty, but opposition to China's version of capitalism is starting to become more vocal.

Maintaining control of the population, now that so many have moved from the **authoritarian** rule of interior regions to the more liberal-run coastal regions, has become a more pressing political problem facing the government. Its urban citizens increasingly desire more political freedom. At the moment, the Communist Party of China restricts freedom of speech and free elections. It also carries out internet censorship through dozens of internet regulations. In 2003, it completed its Golden Shield Project, nicknamed the 'Great Firewall of China' which ensures that any website content deemed inappropriate can be blocked at the country's six internet gateways. The authorities also monitor internet access by individuals and companies.

Demands for more freedom could escalate at any time, creating a re-run of the Tiananmen Square crisis and massacre of 1989, when the government brutally retaliated against student-led protests, killing hundreds of opponents. Any such protest and response, in the near future, could destabilise the country. Pro-democracy protests in Hong Kong during 2019, a territory which enjoys more autonomy than mainland China under the 'one country, two systems' principle, provide a foretaste of the challenges that lie ahead for the government.

The Economic Challenges Facing China Concluded:

By its very size, China will almost certainly become the largest economy in the world in the not too distant future. Using some measures, it is already. China's Gross National Income (GNI), adjusted for purchasing power parity, was $25.26 trillion in 2018, representing 18% of global output, and putting it ahead of the US by more than $3 trillion. The more interesting aspect will be about the consequences of its slowing economic growth. According to the Peterson Institute for International Economics, each 1% drop in Chinese growth is likely to take 0.2% off global growth. The ramifications will be felt all around the world, creating far-reaching political, economic, social and environmental challenges. Napoleon once said "China is a sleeping giant. Let her sleep, for when she wakes she will shake the world." These famous words are coming true today, as China's emergence into an economic superpower enables it to shape and dictate the global economic system, thereby influencing the fortunes of all of us.

Quick Questions:
- *What factors have contributed recently to the risk of an overheated Chinese economy?*
- *Why is there scepticism about the reliability of China's economic data?*
- *How is the Chinese government trying to control the amount of lending by financial institutions?*
- *What is the problem with China's reliance on so many state-owned factories?*
- *What was China's GDP growth in 2019?*
- *Why does China need to shift its economy towards the high-tech sector?*
- *How many Chinese students graduated in 2019?*
- *What industries does China wish to grow under its 'Made in China 2025' plan?*
- *How did China's trade surplus with the US change between 2017 and 2018?*
- *Why did the US government ban Huawei from using the technology of American firms?*
- *How is the Belt and Road Initiative expected to benefit China?*
- *What are the implications of China's growing demand for energy?*
- *What did China attract 138 million of in 2016?*
- *What is the significance of the Golden Shield Project?*

Tasks & Discussion:
- *How valid are the concerns about the sustainability of China's economy?*
- *What political challenges are likely to emerge in China if annual GDP growth falls as low as 4%?*
- *How has China's car industry demonstrated it can compete successfully with foreign car manufacturers?*
- *How can foreign manufacturers compete successfully with Chinese manufacturers?*
- *Outline the factors which lie behind the recent trade and technology disputes between China and the USA.*
- *What makes China different to all other NICs?*

Chapter 4: China's Role Abroad

China's growing global influence has not just been the result of its emergence as the 'workshop to the world'. As well as its export-led manufacturing sector, the country has become a major importer of minerals, energy and foodstuffs. Not surprisingly, China has been engaged in many deals with other countries, to ensure reliable access to these essential goods. In addition, China has been investing its surplus foreign exchange reserves in a wide range of strategic projects abroad. To a certain extent, China's alliances with other developing countries, especially those in Africa, are changing the dynamics of the world order. Nevertheless, China is also looking to develop partnerships with the advanced economies too, recognising that their markets provide huge potential for investment.

As the world's second largest economy, the fastest growing economy (alongside India) in the Group of Twenty (**G20**), and with several trillion dollars of foreign exchange reserves, China has a considerable amount of cash to invest abroad. In 2005, China invested around $17 billion in global assets, a figure dwarfed by the $120 billion it invested in 2018. 57% of this investment came from privately-owned Chinese companies. In the context of global trade, or the economic output of the more advanced economies, the latest figure is still fairly small, but all the signs point to further substantial increases over the coming years and decades. Just as the Chinese economy has grown at breakneck speed since the 1990s, so China's investment abroad has accelerated, and is likely to prove unstoppable despite the country's recent economic slowdown.

Belt and Road Initiative:

This global infrastructure scheme was officially launched in September 2013 by President Xi Jinping in a speech advocating the creation of a 'Silk Road Economic Belt'. The project was later expanded and re-branded as the 'Belt and Road Initiative' (BRI).

The BRI has two major features. Firstly, the 'Silk Road Economic Belt' (the belt) consists of a series of overland corridors connecting China with Europe, via Central Asia and the Middle East. Secondly, the '21st Century Maritime Silk Road' (the road) is not actually a road but rather a sea route linking China's southern coast to east Africa and the Mediterranean.

China's 'Belt and Road Initiative', incorporating the 'Silk Road Economic Belt' and the '21ˢᵗ Century Maritime Silk Road'. (Image: © Mpavlov | Dreamstime.com)

*The BRI appears to be an immensely ambitious economic development campaign through which China hopes to boost trade and stimulate economic growth across Asia and beyond, with potential benefits for dozens of countries in the region. At the same time, China stands to gain from the opening up of new markets for Chinese goods and technology, and the ability to exercise **soft power** from its dominant geopolitical influence across Asia. The Chinese government plans to ultimately lend as much as $8 trillion for infrastructure in 68 countries, with much of the funds coming from the China Development Bank. In fact, the scheme has become a* *global project, expanding far beyond its original core of Eurasia and the Middle East, to include New Zealand, the Arctic, Africa and Latin America.*

Chinese companies set to gain from future trade are those involved in transport and telecoms, helping them to grow into global brands. Chinese manufacturing also stands to gain, including steel and other heavy industries struggling from current overcapacity.

At least $900 billion of projects have been planned or are currently underway since the 2013 launch, leading analysts to predict that the initiative will surpass the investments made under the US' post-war Marshall reconstruction plan. More than 130 countries have signed deals or expressed interest in the BRI. Critics of the BRI claim that it will saddle poor countries with unmanageable debts.

Of the specific projects so far, probably the largest investment has been the creation of the 'China-Pakistan Economic Corridor', a $62 billion scheme involving motorways, power plants, wind farms, factories and railway lines. Other schemes include the Mombasa-Nairobi railway in Kenya, the China-Laos railway, the China-Thailand railway and the Jakarta-Bandung high-speed railway in Indonesia.

However, some countries have rejected investment linked to the BRI. Chinese-funded projects have been cancelled or suspended in Sierra Leone, Nepal, Myanmar and Malaysia amid concerns over debt, corruption and political meddling. In Sri Lanka, a long-time ally of China, arguments over China's political and economic influence contributed to the fall of the government in 2015. A $1.1 billion port project that was opened at Hambantota in 2010, and funded by China, had to be handed back by the Sri Lankan government on a 99-year lease to China, in 2017, due to mounting debts.

Outstanding loans on China's overseas lending have risen to more than $700 billion today. In response to criticisms that its lending is exploiting vulnerable LICs by creating 'debt traps' that ultimately benefit China's political and military ambitions, President Xi has signalled that his government will monitor future lending more *closely, much of which comes from state-owned enterprises. A greater focus on higher-quality projects and a crackdown on corruption have been promised to protect the reputation of the BRI.*

It is still early days for the BRI, so whether it helps China achieve its goal of kick-starting 'a new era of globalisation', spreading wealth and prosperity to many LICs and NICs at the same time, remains to be seen.

China in Africa and South America:

China has been keen to develop a new economic relationship with the continents of Africa, South America and Asia. Chinese companies, many of them state-owned, are pouring the country's huge foreign exchange reserves into projects and deals with overseas companies that will bring China cheap access to minerals, energy and foodstuffs.

The result of China's hunger for energy and resources, is that it is shifting the global balance of power, and inevitably coming into conflict with the major players from the developed world. China's 'invasion of Africa', in particular, has triggered critical comments from some of the leaders of the world's advanced economies. China is now the largest financier of infrastructure in Africa, funding 20% of projects on the continent, as well as constructing an even greater number. There is concern about the country's growing global influence, and the sustainability for African nations of the deals being struck with China. The small African nation of Djibouti has received $1.4 billion from China, representing more than 75% of its GDP. Its coastal location provides China's BRI with a foothold on the continent, but repaying the debt will not be straightforward. It is not yet certain whether this 21st century form of 'colonialism' is any better than the colonialism of old.

China's leading role in Africa is naturally being driven by economic necessity. As well as purchasing raw materials, such as oil, iron ore and copper, China is also investing in companies, building essential infrastructure, and increasing its cultural influence. According to the management consultancy firm, McKinsey, there are around 10,000

Chinese businesses operating in Africa. Trade deals have been signed with more than 40 African countries, including a number governed by questionable regimes.

Raw materials from Africa are vital in allowing China to maintain, and extend, its extraordinary manufacturing capacity. However, some will end up back in Africa, in the form of cheap vehicles, machinery and footwear. These will potentially flood African markets, thereby threatening the growth of local industries, and contributing to a balance of trade deficit. Trade between Africa and China now exceeds $70 billion a year, more than 15 times the figure from a decade earlier.

China has also provided billions of dollars in loans to African states, thereby extending its political, and not just economic, influence over the continent. For example, Nigeria has taken out oil-backed loans from China to finance new gas-fired power stations. In Kenya, the $3.8 billion Mombasa-Nairobi express railway, essential to speed up the movement of goods and people from the coast to the inland capital, was completed in 2017. It was built by China Road and Bridge Corporation, a state-owned construction company, and funded by borrowing from the Export-Import Bank of China. A second section linking Nairobi to Naivasha was opened in 2019. The eventual plan is to connect six other East African countries, opening the region to international trade. However, China's more cautious approach to BRI projects since early 2019 has led to a delay in funding the extension of the railway to Uganda due to concerns over Kenya's ability to service its debts.

Similarly, Chinese companies are involved in the Sicomines deal in Congo, a controversial $6.5 billion mega-deal agreed in 2007 which has seen Chinese companies spending more than $400 million on roads, schools and hospitals. This investment is in exchange for a share of the mining wealth from extracting copper and cobalt, in a joint venture with Congo's state mining agency. Deals, such as this, offer better terms for African governments and companies than Western companies typically offer. Yet, China gains even more from negotiating an exemption from taxes until its loans are repaid, while simultaneously gaining guaranteed access to minerals crucial for electric vehicle batteries and consumer electronics products.

China has also been at the forefront of encouraging African countries to establish export-focused Special Economic Zones, similar in scope to the SEZs that have proved so successful in China. The first Chinese-initiated SEZ was established in Zambia in 2007, and others have followed, such as in Ethiopia, Djibouti, Rwanda and Nigeria, with China providing much of the initial infrastructure investment. The processing of raw materials is the dominant industry, but some labour-intensive manufacturing is starting to appear. The benefits for China are clear. As well as gaining access to lucrative raw materials required by its own industries, China is also able to off-load some of its more polluting industries to Africa.

It is no coincidence that Africa's fastest growing economies are those that are receiving unparalleled levels of foreign direct investment from China. In 2012 alone, China invested $15 billion in Nigeria, $6 billion in the Democratic Republic of Congo, and $5 billion in Niger. These investments ensure that the African countries gain a chance to secure long-term development. But, they do carry a risk. More than a million Chinese have moved to Africa since the trade boom began, and Chinese workers are restricting the employment opportunities of locals. However, China does appear to be committed to the long-term development of the SEZs in Africa, with money made available for both large factories and smaller African enterprises to become established in the zones.

China's drive into South America has been another example of the increasing number of 'south-south' alliances that it has forged with other developing countries. These partnerships, between countries outside the established group of advanced economies of the 'north', are changing the established world order. China's investment in Brazil is worth up to $40 billion a year. In 2009, the Brazilian energy company, Petrobras, agreed a $10 billion loan deal with China's

Development Bank. As part of the deal, China gets a guaranteed quota of oil from Petrobras.

The construction of a huge port and industrial complex in Brazil, the £1.6 billion Superporto do Acu, is a further visible sign of China's push into South America. The port's huge two-mile long pier, the 'Highway to China', enables the Chinese to meet their thirst for iron ore, crude oil and soya from Brazil. China's state-owned Wuhan Iron and Steel Corporation (WISCO) planned to build a $5 billion steel plant at the port to process some of the raw material, although this was eventually shelved.

Carajas, in Brazil's Amazonia region, provides a huge source of high-quality iron ore which China has been keen to get its hands on. Yet, the environment is being hit twice. Not only is the mining itself a threat to the rainforest, but also the use of charcoal in the blast furnaces of the nearby iron and steel plant is contributing to the problem of deforestation.

In addition, China is increasing its export business in the South American market, which is bringing some less favourable economic consequences for Brazil. The combination of an undervalued renminbi (yuan), and a surging Brazilian real, has led to a flood of low-price Chinese goods impacting on Brazilian manufacturers of clothes, fabrics, toys and utensils.

China in Europe, the UK and USA:

Despite China's interest in Africa, South America and Asia, the advanced economies of North America and Europe are also on its radar, and increased co-operation can bring mutual benefits. China's state-run companies and banks, as well as its largest **sovereign wealth fund** (China Investment Corporation), with assets exceeding $900 billion, are all investing overseas. Chinese investments in Europe soared to almost $40 billion in 2016, before contracting in 2017 and 2018. Italy, in 2019, became the first G7 country to sign a memorandum to join the BRI, despite pressure from some EU countries and the US. More than 20 other European countries have also signed up to the BRI.

The UK is the largest recipient of Chinese FDI in Europe. Over the past nine years, China's investments in Britain have been equivalent to 0.7% of the UK's total GDP. The UK government has been looking to increase this investment, by encouraging closer economic and trade ties with Asia's largest economy.

"We want a golden relationship with China that will help foster a golden decade for this country. Simply put, we want to make the UK China's best partner in the west." (George Osbourne, Chancellor of the Exchequer 19.09.15)

Discussions between China and Britain have centred around a possible multi-billion-pound investment by the state-owned China Development Bank (CDB) in strategic transport and energy projects, such as new nuclear plants and the proposed high-speed (HS2) rail project. At the end of 2013, the two countries agreed a jointly funded £200 million UK-China Research and Innovation Partnership, as well as an initiative to boost their digital and media industries, that could be worth £2 billion. In 2014, BP secured a $20 billion deal with China National Offshore Oil Corporation to supply it with liquefied natural gas. In total, Chinese companies were responsible for more than £4 billion worth of FDI in Britain in 2015.

Further trade deals, worth in excess of £35 billion, were struck in October 2015, during the visit to Britain of China's leader, Xi Jinping. The most important strategic deal for the UK was an agreement between the government, EDF Energy and China General Nuclear Power Corporation (CGN) that will see CGN take a one-third stake in a new nuclear power plant at Hinkley Point, Somerset for an investment of £6 billion. Other deals were agreed between the UK and China to help unlock the potential of the so-called '**Northern Powerhouse**', a concept launched by Chancellor George Osbourne in 2014. The idea was to utilise Chinese investment in infrastructure projects to help boost northern cities and rebalance the UK's economy from its overdependence on London and the South-East.

For China, northern England appeals as part of its BRI to boost trade with one of Europe's largest economies.

In 2015, Britain's Prime Minister, David Cameron, claimed that "no country in the world is more open to Chinese investment than the UK". Chinese companies already hold stakes in many large UK organisations. China Investment Corporation (CIC), the sovereign wealth fund, has financial interests in Canary Wharf, Heathrow Airport and Thames Water. Geely, the Chinese automaker, owns Manganese Bronze, the London black cab maker.

Dalian Wanda's acquisition of Sunseeker, famous for providing yachts for James Bond movies, will help Sunseeker to exploit the growing market in China for luxury yachts. (Image: © Adrian Pingstone, Wikimedia, CC)

In early 2014, it was announced that China's largest privately-owned property developer, Dalian Wanda, would be investing up to £3 billion in urban regeneration projects across the UK. The company will be adding to its growing portfolio in the country. In 2013, Dalian Wanda splashed out more than £700 million for an upmarket hotel and residential development on the South Bank in London; as well as buying Sunseeker, the UK's leading luxury yacht maker, for £320 million.

The arrival of the first freight train from China to the UK in January 2017, transporting 34 containers of high street goods, was a symbolic moment in China's push to create a new 'Silk Road Economic Belt' (part of its BRI) connecting Eastern Asia with Europe. The journey from the city of Yiwu, on China's east coast, to London covered 12,000 kilometres, crossed 7 countries and took 18 days to complete. The freight train operator claims that the cost of rail freight is half that of air cargo, and cuts two weeks off the journey time by container ship. The freight train returned to China with goods from the UK. Whether this marks the beginning of a new era of trade between the two countries remains to be seen.

Chinese Investment in the UK:

Northumbrian Water - takeover of company for £2.4 billion by Cheung Kong Infrastructure (CKI) in 2011

Sunseeker International - majority stake purchased for £320 million by Dalian Wanda in 2013

Heathrow Airport - 10% stake purchased for £450 million by the sovereign wealth fund, China Investment Corporation (CIC), in 2009

Thames Water - 9% stake purchased for an estimated £500 million by the sovereign wealth fund, China Investment Corporation (CIC), in 2012

Barclays Bank - 3% stake purchased for £1.5 billion by China Development Bank in 2007

BP - 1% stake purchased for £1 billion by the sovereign wealth fund, State Administration of Foreign Exchange (SAFE), in 2008

Three (mobile network operator) - owned by CK Hutchison Holdings (Hutchison Whampoa) since 2003

Britain's large and open financial system has also seen London become the main centre, outside of China and Hong Kong, for trading and transacting in the renminbi (yuan). Co-operation between the two countries could strengthen the possibility of China being able to secure a free-trade agreement, especially with the UK officially exiting the EU on 31st January 2020.

Chinese investment in the US increased dramatically in 2015, to reach $23 billion, largely due to acquisitions in the financial services, business services, hospitality and real estate sectors. Although earlier investment was mostly driven by state-owned enterprises, more than 70% of the latest investment has come from privately-owned Chinese companies. Despite resistance in the past by the US government, there is now a growing acceptance that the influx of foreign capital into the country's real estate can be beneficial. For example, investment by Chinese companies has targeted declining urban and industrial centres in the north, such as Detroit, places that other investors have deserted. Furthermore, this inward investment is a sign of China's growing integration into the global market.

Yet, not all Chinese money has been so welcome. Concerns about computer security impacting on national security have hindered attempts by China's Huawei Technologies to buy assets in the US. Another worry is that investment from highly subsidised Chinese state-owned enterprises will expand the influence of China's government, or distort market competition.

Growth of Huawei and Concerns Abroad:

Huawei is a Chinese TNC that manufactures telecommunications equipment and consumer electronics. In 2018, it became the world's second-biggest smartphone-maker, behind South Korea's Samsung, having overtaken Apple. It is a major player in the development of the infrastructure for the lightning-fast 5G mobile networks that will transform mobile internet connectivity and facilitate a huge rise in 'Internet of Things' technology, enabling a smarter and more connected world. Its major rivals in the provision of 5G network infrastructure are the two Scandinavian companies, Ericsson and Nokia.

Huawei's HQ is located in Shenzhen, Guangdong province. The company was founded in 1987 by Ren Zhengfei, a former engineer in the Chinese People's Liberation Army. Originally, a manufacturer of phone switches, its expansion into manufacturing state-of-the-art telecommunications network equipment and smartphones has seen the company grow rapidly. It was ranked the 72nd largest TNC in the 2018 edition of the Fortune Global 500 Index, an increase of 11 places on the previous year, with annual revenue at $89 billion generating a $7 billion profit. Huawei has promised to spend at least 15% of its annual revenue on research and development to maintain its global competitiveness. It works with some of the world's largest telecoms operators, including BT and Vodafone. The company has around 180,000 employees and operates in more than 170 countries.

Although Huawei is a private Chinese company, owned by its employees, foreign governments in the West have expressed concern that the Chinese government, which has significant influence over all business activity in China, could use Huawei as a proxy to access sensitive political and economic information via its installed telecommunications network equipment which accounts for around 30% of the global market. Critics suggest that the Chinese government could order the firm to allow backdoor access to its devices to enable hack attacks on critical network infrastructure, eavesdrop on conversations or gain high-level access to sensitive data.

To date, the US, New Zealand and Australia have barred Huawei from involvement in their next-generation (5G) mobile networks over cybersecurity concerns. The UK has restricted the involvement of Huawei by keeping its equipment away from the core of its 5G network, and from infrastructure to be used by the emergency services.

Controversy has also surrounded Huawei's chief financial officer, Meng Wanzhou, daughter of the company's founder. In December

2018, she was arrested in Canada on behalf of the US, and subsequently charged by the US with fraud and the circumventing of American sanctions on trade with Iran.

The US government's opposition to Huawei has been strongest among the G20 nations. In May 2019, the Trump administration added Huawei to a list of companies that US firms cannot trade with unless they have a licence. Huawei spends more than $10 billion annually on software, processors and other components from American firms. However, two 90-day temporary extensions followed, enabling Google, Intel, Qualcomm and other US tech firms to continue their business with Huawei. The extensions add weight to the argument that Huawei is being used as a bargaining chip in the on-going US-China trade war.

Cheap exports from China have also been a source of discontent in both the US and Europe. Western steel producers have been hugely impacted by low-price steel from China, arising from its overcapacity. China produces more than half of the world's steel, and has been accused of manipulating the steel market, through currency manipulation and state subsidies. The US has imposed higher tariffs on specific types of steel from China, and European steel producers have demanded similar tariff protection.

China's Role Abroad Concluded:

Despite the inevitable fears arising from China's rapid export growth, and the risk of unsustainable debts for low-income countries linked to the BRI; the more that Chinese companies invest abroad, the more they have a reason to become partners rather than simply competitors. Between 2005 and 2013, China spent around $700 billion in overseas investments. This is a financial commitment that it will not wish to jeopardise. As such, it should be in China's interest to see the economies of these countries continuing to grow.

Tasks & Discussion:

- *Why have some Western governments been critical of China's growing influence in Africa?*
- *Why do many African governments view China's involvement in the continent more favourably?*
- *To what extent is a 'China-Brazil' alliance beneficial for both countries?*
- *Discuss the pros and cons of China's Belt and Road Initiative.*
- *How does the UK benefit from being open to Chinese investment?*
- *Discuss the social, economic and political issues that China's rapid economic growth has created for other countries.*

Chapter 5: China's Environmental Legacy

China's obsession with economic growth has been to the detriment of its own environment, and the health of its citizens. The country's dependence on coal, as an energy source, has been a major cause of its heavily polluted air, and a factor in the estimated deaths prematurely of a quarter of a million people each year. Furthermore, industrial and vehicle emissions push the number of air pollution victims to more than a million annually. If that was not enough, the Chinese people have to contend with water shortages, contaminated water supplies, dangerous factory conditions and toxic products. Environmental problems are slowly being addressed by the Chinese government, and investment in green technologies promises a less harmful future.

China's rush into economic expansion has taken a heavy toll on its environment. Government priorities have been on economic growth, with environmental protection well down the order. In the hunt for profits and market share, factories and power stations have also routinely ignored the government's lax environmental rules. The outcome is that the people of China are paying a heavy environmental and health price for the country's breath-taking economic growth. Air pollution is thought to cut the life expectancy of people living in northern China by five years.

The signs of an environment under severe stress are visible throughout the country. Heavily polluted air, toxic land, contaminated lakes, poisoned rivers and unsafe drinking water are features of both urban and rural areas. Roadsides everywhere are blanketed with discarded plastic bags and bottles. International concerns have arisen too, since China is the world's largest emitter of greenhouse gases, as well as a major exporter of acid rain pollution. Furthermore, Greenpeace claim that China is the biggest driver of rainforest destruction, with 50% of all rainforest logs destined for China.

Air Pollution:

Pollution levels are exacerbated by the fact that China relies on coal for almost 60% of its energy, producing just under 9 million tonnes of sulphur dioxide in 2017, a major contributor to the damaging ecological impacts from acid rain. China's own people suffer just as acutely as the natural environment. Research, commissioned by Greenpeace, claims that China's 2,300 coal-burning plants caused 257,000 premature deaths in 2011. Coal emissions were also responsible for 320,000 children suffering from asthma, 340,000 hospital admissions, and 141 million days of sick leave.

Smog is a near-daily occurrence in Chongqing due to the city's heavy industries and nearby coal-burning plants. Dozens of other cities in China fare even worse than Chongqing. (Image: ID 122081278 © Plej92 | Dreamstime.com)

A World Health Organization report estimated that just over 1 million Chinese died prematurely in 2012 due to air pollution as a whole, which includes emissions from industry and transport, as well as the coal power sector. In addition, the World Bank estimates that the health costs of air and water pollution in China amount to 4.3% of its GDP. This figure rises to 5.8% of GDP when non-health costs, such as loss of crops, loss of fisheries and material damage, are taken into account. More than half of the proposed coal-burning plants are to be built in areas of high water stress. If these plants are built, they could further strain already-scarce resources, threatening water security for China's farms and communities in particular. Clearly, China is paying a huge price for the lack of pollution controls placed on the factories and businesses that are driving its economy.

In 2011, China's Ministry of Environmental Protection rated the air quality in 45 of the country's major cities as being poor. Beijing was rated particularly poor, due to emissions from the city's near 5 million cars, as well as its coal-burning factories and homes. For days on end, a yellow-brown smog can hide the skyscrapers of Beijing. The use of low-grade fuel is part of the problem. Nitrous oxide emissions in the city are particularly high, causing irritation to people's lungs, and lowering their resistance to respiratory infections.

The authorities in Beijing have attempted to control air pollution, by limiting both car purchases and car use. There are daily restrictions on cars, linked to licence plate numbers. During the run-up to the 2008 Olympics in Beijing, there were huge efforts to clean up the city. A number of the heavy-polluting factories were relocated away from the city. Half the city's cars were banned each day, while the older, more polluting cars were taken off the streets permanently. Yet, despite all these measures, the city's chronic pollution problem has not gone away.

In February 2014, Beijing, and the surrounding provinces, endured more than a week of particularly dense smog, which Chinese scientists reported was so bad that its effects were comparable to a 'nuclear winter'. Beijing's concentration of PM 2.5 particles, which are small enough to penetrate deep into the lungs and enter the bloodstream, hit 505 micrograms per cubic metre. This is more than 20 times the safe level recommended by the World Health Organization.

Road space rationing in Beijing has been made permanent since its introduction for the 2008 Summer Olympics. The end number on the licence plate determines which day of the week the vehicle cannot be used inside the city's 5th Ring Road. (Image: © Peter Lowe)

The worsening air pollution created a significant economic and social toll. Over 140 factories had their production suspended or cut, while further precautions included the grounding of flights, and the closing of schools, highways and tourist attractions. The smog was observed to be slowing photosynthesis in plants; and similar conditions, over an extended period of time, could significantly harm the country's agricultural production. The relocation of polluting industries to the countryside means that factory towers, belching smoke above green paddy fields, are a common sight in the rural areas.

In response to the recurring air pollution problem in Beijing, around 30% of which comes from vehicle exhaust fumes, the government announced that 300,000 of the city's older and high-polluting vehicles would be decommissioned in 2014. In addition, 294 polluting factories were closed, or removed, during the same year.

For 2015, there were plans to shut down 300 factories and retire 200,000 vehicles. Elsewhere in China, investment in electric buses and taxis has helped to reduce levels of urban air pollution. All 16,000 buses in Shenzhen became electric-powered by 2018, and all the city's taxis were required to be electric too. More than 30 Chinese cities have made plans to achieve 100% electrified public transit by 2020.

Cleaner electric buses are becoming a more common sight in Beijing. By 2017, there were nearly 14,000 new buses, powered by electricity or natural gas, halving the current carbon emissions from the city's bus fleet. (Image: © Peter Lowe)

Water Pollution:

Another major problem is the lack of clean water. 700 million Chinese drink water contaminated with human and animal waste. Only 10% of the estimated 20 billion tonnes of raw sewage, generated by homes and businesses in the cities, is treated. The rest is dumped straight into rivers and lakes, with the result that 90% of the waterways in urban areas are heavily polluted. Another report, by the Ministry of Environmental Protection, found that the Haihe River, in northern China, was the country's filthiest river. The people living in China's northern provinces do seem to be bearing the brunt of the environmental abuses arising from industrialisation, as illustrated by the notorious incident in Harbin, Jilin province, in November 2005.

An industrial explosion, that killed six workers and injured dozens more, at a petrochemical plant in Jilin province led to a massive water contamination problem for the north-eastern city of Harbin, which is situated downstream of the affected Jilin City. The accident flooded the Songhua River with more than 100 tonnes of toxic fluid, including benzene and nitrobenzene, leaving nearly 4 million people without drinking water for five days.

The authorities attempted to cover up the problem for ten days after the explosion, and residents of Harbin were initially told that their water supply was being shut for routine maintenance. Trucks had to transport huge quantities of water to the city from other parts of China. Benzene levels in the river reached 100 times their national safety levels, although the decision to shut off the water supply prevented further deaths or illnesses among Harbin's population.

Another near environmental disaster occurred at Jilin in 2010, when floods washed several thousand drums of chemicals from two petrochemical plants into the Songhua River. Toxic chemicals were present, and the authorities had to deploy the army to recover the drums. The chemicals were eventually removed from the river, although three soldiers lost their lives. Despite the potential chemical risk, the authorities claimed that the water remained safe for drinking throughout the ordeal.

Soil Pollution:

Soil pollution has received less publicity than air and water pollution, but it poses just as big a threat to the health of China's citizens. Data on soil pollution has been a closely guarded secret until recently. In February 2013, China's MEP finally admitted that 'cancer villages' existed in the country. It is believed that there are as many as 450 such villages, the result of the industrialisation of the countryside that has contaminated nearby farmland with cadmium, lead, mercury and other heavy metals.

One of the worst affected areas surrounds Lake Tai, in Central China's Jiangsu and Zhejiang provinces. Since the 1990s, nearly 3,000 factories have been built around the lake, more than 30% of them producing toxic chemicals. The effect for many years has been the poisoning of both the lake and the surrounding fields. Only in the last few years have the authorities started to rectify the damage by closing down the worst-offending chemical plants.

Toxic Products:

The dash for profits has had other unpleasant health consequences, some with potentially global effects. The American toy manufacturer, Mattel, closed its last factory in the United States in 2002, outsourcing its production to China. This began a chain of events that led to the 'toxic toys' scandal, involving lead contamination. In 2007, Mattel was forced to recall over 18 million products, due to the surface paint coatings containing amounts of lead that exceeded international limits.

The Chinese milk scandal of 2008 broke out after 16 infants, in Gansu province, who had been fed on milk powder, were diagnosed with kidney stones. The state-owned Sanlu Group dairy company was responsible for melamine-tainting, although a number of other Chinese companies were found to have also used the chemical melamine, in their milk and infant formula, to increase its protein content. The polluted milk led to the deaths of six infants, the hospitalisation of 50,000 babies, and a total of 300,000 victims.

The issue raised concerns about food safety and political corruption in China, and damaged the country's food exports. A spokesman from the World Health Organization claimed that the scale of the problem proved it was "a large-scale intentional activity to deceive consumers for simple, basic, short-term profits."

Other Health & Safety Concerns:

Lead poisoning was diagnosed in 2009 in hundreds of children living near the Dongling Lead and Zinc Smelting Company plant in Shaanxi province. The plant was opened in 2003, but parents discovered their children suffering from nose bleeds and memory problems. 851 children were found to have excessive lead poisoning, including 174 serious cases requiring hospitalisation. Lead concentrations were up to ten times safe levels. The government responded to the mass poisonings by ordering the closure of the plant.

The human cost of China's rapid industrial expansion is also illustrated by the country's workplace death rate, which is twelve times higher than in the UK. Assembly-line workers are much more likely to be operating machinery without safety guards, or spraying paint with inadequate face masks. Independent trade unions are banned by the government, so workers have little chance of their grievances being heard and acted upon.

Tianjin Explosions:

On 12th August 2015, a series of explosions occurred at the Port of Tianjin. The initial blast was from hazardous chemicals stored in a collection of warehouses owned by Ruihai International Logistics. The first explosion registered as a magnitude 2.3 earthquake, equivalent to 3 tonnes of TNT, but this was followed within 30 seconds by a second and more powerful explosion, equivalent to 21 tonnes of TNT. Fireballs from these explosions reached hundreds of metres into the sky.

The death toll exceeded 170 people, at least half of whom were firefighters. Around 800 people were injured. The explosions blasted shipping containers, and incinerated thousands of new vehicles, production facilities and dormitories.

The explosions generated insurance losses of between $1.5 and $3 billion. Many of the 5,800 destroyed vehicles, stored at Tianjin, *belonged to Jaguar Land Rover, impacting on the company's Chinese sales at the time.*

Less clear are the health consequences for the residents of the area. Residents within 3km of the site were ordered to evacuate when it became clear that highly toxic sodium cyanide was being stored at the port. Government officials insisted that air and water quality levels were safe, while simultaneously sending anti-chemical warfare troops to the site of the explosions.

The explosions have raised further questions in China, and the wider world, over the country's industrial safety record, and the precautions adopted in city planning. Of particular concern was that residential buildings were allowed within 1km of the Ruihai warehouses that stored dangerous chemicals, President Xi Jinping urged the authorities to learn the "extremely profound" lessons from the disaster, and ensure that China followed a path of "safe growth".

There are signs that China's environmental consciousness is improving, and spending on environmental and health protection has increased in recent years, along with more rigorous enforcing of environmental and safety laws. The government now publishes figures for air quality in all its major cities, and is committed to spending $275 billion over the next five years to tackle the problem. For the past few decades, the government promoted economic growth to keep its people content. But, now that people have higher incomes, they are starting to worry about their quality of life, and the outcome is unrest and protest. This is forcing the government to take more action. Indeed, air pollution is now viewed as a national disaster by the government. In March 2015, President Xi promised "to punish, with an iron hand, any violators who destroy ecology or environment, with no exceptions."

Japan has provided financial and technological assistance, motivated by the fact that it suffers from the downwind acid rain effects from China's dependency on coal. More of China's coal-fired power stations are now using cleaner coal technology. In late 2013, the government announced a ban on new coal-fired power plants in the three most important metropolitan areas around Beijing, Shanghai, and Guangzhou. This is yet a further sign that the authorities are taking steps to reverse the damage done by decades of manufacturing-driven growth. As China continues to transition to lower emission coal-burning technologies and increase its energy production from renewable sources, levels of sulphur dioxide, fine particulate matter (PM 2.5) and ozone should continue their recent fall.

For China, the benefits of greater environmental awareness are that it should stimulate its own companies to become internationally competitive in emerging green technologies. Equally, there has been growing awareness of the rising health costs from exposure to outdoor pollutants and also to aerosols in the workplace, that have contributed to more people suffering from chronic breathing problems, bronchitis and lung cancer. The downside for China is that stronger environmental laws will push up the costs of production, eroding some of the comparative advantage that the country offers to companies.

China's Environmental Legacy Concluded:

China's rapid transformation into an industrial powerhouse has brought huge environmental costs to the country. Although these were largely ignored in the past as the country prioritised getting rich, recent developments suggest a significant shift in opinion on environmental matters, translating into improved monitoring and stronger law enforcement. China has also played a key role in removing and recycling much of the waste generated by the mass consumption of the largest HICs. Until 2017, the containers delivering exported consumer goods from China were used to return waste plastic, packaging and other materials back to China for reprocessing. Unsurprisingly, China is now refusing some of this imported waste as it considers more fully the impact on its own environment. Furthermore, around one-third of all Chinese carbon emissions are the result of producing exports for consumption by the advanced economies of the world. One positive side-effect of the temporary shutdown of China's industries during the coronavirus pandemic of 2020 was the noticeable improvement in air quality across its cities. China's environmental record may not be among the best in the world, but it is far from being the only nation that needs to implement stronger policies to ensure resources are used more sustainably.

Tasks & Discussion:
- *Why is air pollution such a serious problem in China?*
- *Outline the social and economic impacts of China's heavily polluted air.*
- *Discuss the causes of Beijing's pollution problems.*
- *How has the government attempted to tackle Beijing's pollution problems, and with what degree of success?*
- *Why is water quality poor in many parts of China?*
- *Outline the evidence that consumer safety has been affected by corruption and the drive for profits in China.*
- *To what extent are the environmental costs of China's economic growth more acute in urban than rural areas?*
- *How is China demonstrating a greater degree of environmental awareness in recent years?*
- *What are the pros and cons for China of implementing stronger environmental protection?*

Examples of Exam-Style Questions on China, Development & Globalisation Issues:
- *Explain the recent growth of industries in China.*
- *Examine the impact of NICs on the global economy.*
- *Outline the reasons for the growth of TNCs.*
- *Assess the economic and social impacts of TNCs.*
- *Discuss the impacts of TNCs on their host countries.*
- *Evaluate the consequences of globalisation.*
- *Outline the core-periphery relationship that exists in China.*
- *Discuss government policies to address the core-periphery differences in China.*
- *Discuss the importance of TNCs and NICs in the global economy. (essay)*
- *To what extent are NICs the driving force behind globalisation? (essay)*

Chapter 6: China Multiple-Choice Questions

1 How does the size of China's economy (measured in GDP) rank globally today?
a Largest
b Second largest
c Third largest
d Fourth largest

2 Which of these was not a feature of China, under the leadership of Mao Zedong?
a Famines and poverty
b State-owned industries
c Foreign direct investment
d Agricultural-based economy

3 When was the 'one-child' policy introduced?
a 1971
b 1979
c 1989
d 1991

4 Which of these was not a reform introduced by Deng Xiaoping?
a Rural Household Responsibility System
b Joint Venture Law
c Special Economic Zones
d Cultural Revolution

5 China's development strategy has favoured which provinces?
a Eastern provinces
b Western provinces
c Northern provinces
d Inland provinces

6 Which country provided most of the overseas investment in China during the 1980s and 1990s?
a USA
b South Korea
c Japan
d Russia

7 What was the focus of economic development in the Special Economic Zones?
a Energy production
b Consumer industries
c Machine manufacturing
d Raw material extraction

8 Which SEZ enjoyed the most spectacular growth during the 1980s/early 1990s?
a Hong Kong
b Shanghai
c Zhuhai
d Shenzhen

9 Beijing is the most important location in China for which industry?
a Financial services
b Domestic appliances
c Software production
d Motorcycles

10 When did the Tiananmen Square massacre take place?
a 1987
b 1989
c 1991
d 1993

11 Which 'open city' grew quickly during the 1990s, attracting 25% of the foreign direct investment (FDI) in China?
a Hong Kong
b Shanghai
c Beijing
d Tianjin

12 What % of China's soft drinks market was held by Coca-Cola in 2017?
a 8%
b 32%
c 15%
d 24%

13 What % of Apple's global profits came from China in 2017?
a 25%
b 55%
c 5%
d 15%

14 How many people had to be resettled, as a result of the Three Gorges Dam project?
a 2.6 million
b 4.4 million
c 1.2 million
d 3.4 million

15 Which of these is not an important part of Chongqing's economy?
a Motorcycles
b Port facilities
c Heavy industries
d Financial services

16 When did China join the World Trade Organization?
a 1981
b 1991
c 2001
d 2011

17 The biggest source of FDI in China, in recent years, has been from which continent?
a Europe
b South America
c Asia
d North America

18 With which of these countries did China run a trade deficit in 2014?
a Australia
b USA
c Japan
d UK

19 Which Chinese city has the world's 4th largest stock exchange?
a Hong Kong
b Shanghai
c Shenzhen
d Beijing

20 What was the value of FDI in China in 2018?
a $77 billion
b $154 billion
c $94 billion
d $142 billion

21 What % of China's GDP have investment levels, in recent years, reached?
a 15%
b 35%
c 45%
d 65%

22 What was China's total level of debt in 2016?
a 250% of GDP
b 215% of GDP
c 100% of GDP
d 125% of GDP

23 What was the approximate official value of China's GDP in 2019?
a $10 trillion
b $18 trillion
c $6 trillion
d $14 trillion

24 What was the significance for China of 24th August 2015?
a Presidential election
b Economy overtook the US
c Stock market crash
d Silk Road initiative announced

25 What was China's GDP growth in 2019, according to official figures?
a 6.1%
b 1.1%
c 4.1%
d 9.1%

26 What % of China's population still live in rural areas?
a 66%
b 34%
c 41%
d 54%

27 How do wealth levels in China's three richest regions/provinces compare with the three poorest regions/provinces?
a 5-6 times higher
b 3-4 times higher
c 1-2 times higher
d roughly the same

28 Which area has enjoyed the largest reduction in poverty since 2010?
a Tibet
b Yunnan
c Gansu
d Tianjin

29 How many rural labourers moved to the cities between 1979 and 2014?
a 440 million
b 220 million
c 660 million
d 110 million

30 How many people in China have been lifted out of extreme poverty since 1979?
a 100 million
b 200 million
c 400 million
d 80 million

31 Which area has become China's 'Rust Belt', due to two decades of industrial decline?
a North-west
b South-east
c South-west
d North-east

32 Which of these was not an important factor behind the US-China trade war of 2018?
a China's trade surplus
b Belt and Road Initiative
c Intellectual property theft
d National security concerns

33 What % of students go on to higher education in China?
a 80%
b 40%
c 20%
d 50%

34 Which of these is not a Chinese global brand?
a Hyundai
b PetroChina
c Sinopec
d Huawei

35 Which Chinese car manufacturer has a joint venture operation with Jaguar Land Rover?
a SAIC
b Chery
c Dongfeng
d Geely

36 What was the approximate value of China's foreign exchange reserves at the end of 2017?
a $5 trillion
b $12 trillion
c $1 trillion
d $3 trillion

37 Huawei secured a major deal in 2014 with which UK company?
a Dyson
b Vodafone
c Land Rover
d BT

38 Which of these is a long-term consequence of China's 'one-child' policy?
a Youthful population
b Growing workforce size
c Increasing dependency ratio
d Falling pension costs

39 Which of these is not related to the 'Belt and Road Initiative'?
a Lujiazui Finance and Trade Zone
b Silk Road Economic Belt
c China-Pakistan Economic Corridor
d 21st Century Maritime Silk Road

40 What is a key purpose of China's Golden Shield Project?
a Regional connectivity
b Nuclear defence
c Knowledge-based economy
d Internet censorship

41 What % of China's energy requirements comes from coal-burning?
a 45%
b 85%
c 59%
d 71%

42 How many people in China are estimated to die prematurely each year from all sources of air pollution, according to the World Health Organization?
a 600,000
b 250,000
c 2.5 million
d 1 million

43 What is the World Bank's estimate for the health and non-health costs for China arising from the pollution it generates?
a 0.7% of GDP
b 5.8% of GDP
c 2.2% of GDP
d 4.3% of GDP

44 How many cars are used regularly on the roads of Beijing?
a 1 million
b 3 million
c 5 million
d 7 million

45 Which pollutant reached a concentration that was 20 times the safe level over Beijing in early 2014?
a Carbon monoxide
b PM 2.5
c Sulphur dioxide
d Nitrous oxide

46 Which is the most contaminated river in China, according to the Ministry of Environmental Protection?
a Haihe River
b Yangtze River
c Songhua River
d Hwang He River

47 In which Chinese city were 4 million people left without drinking water, following the contamination of its river water?
a Dalian
b Chongqing
c Beijing
d Harbin

48 What was the source of the contamination of the Songhua River in the incident that affected 4 million people?
a Steelworks
b Toy factory
c Petrochemical plant
d Lead & zinc plant

49 What was the toxic substance that forced Mattel to recall over 18 million of its toy products?
a Cadmium
b Lead
c Benzene
d Mercury

50 How many babies were hospitalised by the Chinese milk scandal of 2008?
a 50,000
b 10,000
c 150,000
d 300,000

Answers:
1-b; 2-c; 3-b; 4-d; 5-a; 6-c; 7-b; 8-d; 9-c; 10-b
11-b; 12-c; 13-a; 14-c; 15-d; 16-c; 17-c; 18-a; 19-b; 20-d
21-c; 22-a; 23-d; 24-c; 25-a; 26-c; 27-b; 28-a; 29-b; 30-c
31-d; 32-b; 33-c; 34-a; 35-b; 36-d; 37-b; 38-c; 39-a; 40-d
41-c; 42-d; 43-b; 44-c; 45-b; 46-a; 47-d; 48-c; 49-b; 50-a

Chapter 7: China Economy Timeline

The arrival of a communist government in 1949, under the leadership of Mao Zedong, did little to improve the fortunes of the Chinese. His death in 1976 gave an opportunity for reformers to begin the reinvigoration of the Chinese economy. Under the leadership of Deng Xiaoping, China quickly moved towards a market economy, and continued reforms have dramatically improved the economic condition of the nation. China can now boast a $14 trillion economy, but whether it can sustain its meteoric rise remains to be seen.

China - Key Dates, Events & Statistics

1949 - China becomes a communist country, under the leadership of Mao Zedong

1959-1961 - Great Chinese Famine kills up to 40 million people

1966-1976 - Mao's Cultural Revolution aimed at strengthening communist ideology through the repression of political opponents and capitalists. Up to 2 million deaths

1976 - Death of Mao Zedong

1978 - China starts the move towards a market economy, under the leadership of Deng Xiaoping

1979 - 'One-child' policy introduced

1979 - First Joint Venture Law passed

1980 - First wave of Special Economic Zones established, including Shenzhen

1984 - First wave of Economic and Technological Development Zones established

1989 - Tiananmen Square massacre

1991 - Opening of the Shanghai Stock Exchange. Foreign banks allowed to open branches

1993 - Pudong New Area, opposite the historic city centre of Shanghai, gains special economic status, similar to the other SEZs. The western tip becomes part of the Lujiazui Finance and Trade Zone

2001 - FDI in China reaches $40 billion. China accepted into the World Trade Organisation

2003 - Completion of the Golden Shield Project

2005 - China invests $17 billion abroad

2006 - China becomes the world's largest recipient of FDI. 50% of exports linked to FDI. Economy grows at over 10% per year

2007 - China's GDP exceeds $3 trillion. Per capita GDP around $2,200. Exports worth $1.2 trillion. Richest 10% enjoy 45% of the country's income

2007 - Mattel forced to recall over 18 million toy products, made in China, due to lead contamination

2008 - China's debts reach 125% of GDP. Gini coefficient (measure of inequality) peaks at 0.491

2008 - Chinese milk scandal, caused by the chemical melamine, kills 6 infants and hospitalises 50,000 babies

2009 - Brazilian energy company, Petrobras, agrees a $10 billion loan deal with China's Development Bank

2009-2010 - $400 billion of direct government spending to boost the economy following the Global Financial Crisis

2010 - China's economy surpasses Japan's economy. GDP above $6 trillion

2012 - China's GDP exceeds $8 trillion. Per capita GDP around $6,000. Per capita GDP in Shanghai exceeds $13,000. Domestic investment levels reach 50% of GDP

2012 - China invests $130 billion abroad. $15 billion invested in Nigeria, $6 billion in DR Congo. Trade with Africa worth $70 billion

2012 - WHO report estimates that air pollution leads to 1 million premature deaths in China. All forms of pollution cost 5.8% of GDP

2013 - China invests $14 billion in the US

2013 - Nearly 7 million graduates from China's universities

2013 - President Xi Jinping announces plans for the 'Silk Road Economic Belt', later expanded and re-branded as the 'Belt and Road Initiative'

2014 - FDI in China reaches $128 billion

2014 - BP agrees a $20 billion deal with China National Offshore Oil Corporation to supply it with liquefied natural gas

2015 - Launch of the 'Made in China 2025' development plan. China's GDP reaches $11.07 trillion. GDP growth slows to 6.9%. Exports worth $2.43 trillion. Imports valued at $2.05 trillion

2015 - Chinese-led Asian Infrastructure Investment Bank (AIIB) established

2015 - Shanghai Composite index falls by 8.5% on August 24th as fears of a slowdown in China alarm investors

2016 - End of the 'one-child' policy. GDP growth of 6.7%

2017 - China's GDP exceeds $12 trillion. Exports worth $2.42 trillion. Imports valued at $2.21 trillion. $3.24 trillion of foreign exchange reserves

2018 - President Xi allowed to remain 'president for life' as two-term limit removed. Start of US-China trade war

2018 - China's GDP reaches $13.60 trillion. GDP growth of 6.6%. Per capita GDP of $9,770. Exports worth $2.66 trillion. Imports valued at $2.55 trillion. FDI reaches $142 billion

2019 - Record 8.3 million graduates from China's universities

2019 - Pro-democracy protests occur in Hong Kong, initially in response to a controversial extradition bill

2019 - China's GDP exceeds $14 trillion. GDP growth of just 6.1%, the slowest in almost three decades. Per capita GDP of $10,276

2020 - China and the US sign an agreement to ease the trade war

2020 - Outbreak of a new coronavirus (the SARS-CoV-2 virus and its disease COVID-19) decimates domestic and international trade, business and travel

2020 – Economy contracts by 6.8% in the first quarter of the year due to the coronavirus lockdown

Glossary of Terms

Advanced Economies: Term used by the International Monetary Fund (IMF) to describe high-income countries. Advanced economies have a high level of GDP per capita, score highly on the Human Development Index (HDI), and have a very significant degree of industrialisation.

Authoritarian: Favouring or enforcing strict obedience to authority, at the expense of personal freedom.

Backwash effects: The growth of one particular area (the core) causes people, human capital and physical capital (infrastructure, finance, machines) from other parts of the country (the periphery) to gravitate towards this growing centre. Backwash effects are therefore negative and create regional divergence in social and economic levels of development.

Belt and Road Initiative: Chinese economic development campaign through which China hopes to boost trade and stimulate economic growth across Asia and beyond. The 'Belt' consists of a series of overland corridors connecting China with Europe, via Central Asia and the Middle East. The 'Road' is actually a sea route linking China's southern coast to east Africa and the Mediterranean.

Communist country: Country where the means of production are collectively owned by the society. It has a form of government characterised by single or dominant party rule of a communist party.

Comparative advantages: Factors that enable a country or region to produce particular goods or services at a lower marginal and opportunity cost than other places.

Core-periphery model: Model that seeks to explain a spatial pattern of economic growth, in which one centre or region in a country develops an economic advantage over the rest of the country. The core is the part of a country with the most economic activity and development. The periphery is the area with low or declining economic activity.

Cultural Revolution: Decade-long period of political and social chaos caused by Mao Zedong's attempt to use the Chinese masses to reassert his control over the Communist Party. It began in May 1966, initially through student-led terror (Red Guard divisions) against the country's 'bourgeoisie'. Up to 2 million people died as a consequence of the civil war.

Cumulative causation: The economic principle that multiple changes are set in motion by a single event. The causation might be 'forward' if the effects are positive, as in the case of the location of a new business generating more jobs. The causation would be 'backward' if the effects are negative, such as when a business closed.

Diseconomies (of scale): Higher costs of production that reduce profitability. These may be due to factors such as rising labour costs, worker shortages, higher land costs and tax increases (local, regional or national).

Dumping: The practice that occurs when manufacturers export a product to another country at a price below the price charged in its home market, or below its cost of production.

Economic and Technological Development Zones: Areas with a similar function to SEZs. Many are located within the coastal cities and other open cities inland.

Extreme poverty: Average daily income/consumption of $1.90 or less (at 2015 international prices). Also referred to as absolute poverty, the number of people living in extreme poverty worldwide has been falling since reaching a peak of 1.9 billion in 1990. At the end of 2015, around 700 million people (World Bank figure) continued to suffer from extreme poverty across the world.

Foreign Direct Investment: Investment from one country into another, normally by companies rather than governments, that involves establishing operations or acquiring assets, including stakes in other businesses.

Foreign exchange reserves: Assets held by central banks and monetary authorities, usually in different reserve currencies, mostly the US dollar, and to a lesser extent the Euro, Pound sterling and Japanese yen. Foreign exchange reserves are used to back the liabilities of central banks, such as the local currency issued and the bank reserves deposited with them by the government or financial institutions.

G7: Forum for government ministers from 7 leading economies to meet regularly to discuss issues of mutual or global concern. The members include Canada, France, Germany, Italy, Japan, United Kingdom, United States. The European Union (EU) is also represented. Russia was previously included when the forum existed as the G8, but was excluded from the forum in March 2014, due to its involvement in the Crimea Crisis involving Ukraine.

G20: Group of finance ministers and central bank governors from 20 major economies, that meets regularly to discuss ways to strengthen the global economy, reform international financial institutions and improve financial regulation. The members include Argentina, Australia, Brazil, Canada, China, France, Germany, India, Indonesia, Italy, Japan, Republic of Korea, Mexico, Russia, Saudi Arabia, South Africa, Turkey, United Kingdom, United States, as well as the European Union (EU).

Geopolitical: Impact of geography on politics. In particular, how the geographic location of a country, its size, population, ethnicity, natural resources and technological development can influence the international political behaviour (foreign policy) of other countries, especially neighbouring countries.

Global brands: Brand names of products that have worldwide recognition. A global brand has the advantage of economies of scale in terms of production, recognition and packaging.

Global Financial Crisis: The global financial crisis of 2007/2008 was the largest and most severe financial event since the Great Depression. It resulted in the threat of total collapse of large financial institutions, the bailout of banks by national governments, and downturns in stock markets around the world. Housing markets also suffered, resulting in evictions, and unemployment levels rose. The crisis played a significant role in the failure of key businesses, declines in consumer wealth, and a downturn in economic activity leading to the 2008–2012 global recession.

Great Leap Forward: Mao Zedong's attempt to rapidly industrialise China's peasant economy in the late 1950s. It was an economic and social disaster, responsible for up to 40 million deaths between 1959 and 1961.

Great Western Development Strategy: State-led regional development policy, launched in 2000, with the aim of directing larger amounts of state investment, private capital, loans and foreign direct investment into China's inland provinces and regions.

Gross Domestic Product: The monetary value of all the finished goods and services produced within a country's borders in a specific time period, usually calculated on an annual basis. It includes all private and public consumption, government expenditure, investments, and exports less imports.

Growth poles: Points of economic growth, usually urban locations, and often located in the core region of a country, although governments may try to create new growth poles in the periphery region. Growth poles should interact with surrounding areas, spreading prosperity from the core to the periphery.

High-Income Countries: Countries with high levels of economic development. Typically, they have less than 10% of the workforce in agriculture. They enjoy high levels of nutrition, secondary schooling, literacy, electricity consumption per head, and GNI per capita — above $12,376.

Initial advantages: The advantages which promote early development, growth and further benefits for an area, often leading to the establishment of a core region. Initial advantages include proximity to resources (mineral, agricultural) or favourable locations (natural harbours, route centres).

Knowledge-based economy: Feature of advanced economies where there is greater dependence on knowledge, information and high skill levels, and the increasing need for ready access to all of these by the business and public sectors.

Low-Income Countries: Countries with low levels of economic development. Typically, they have more than 50% of the workforce in agriculture. They suffer from low levels of nutrition, secondary schooling, literacy, electricity consumption per head, and GNI per capita — below $1,026.

Made in China 2025: State-led industrial policy that seeks to make China dominant in global high-tech manufacturing. Industries and sectors targeted include electric cars, next-generation information technology and telecommunications, advanced robotics and artificial intelligence, agricultural technology, aerospace engineering, new synthetic materials, advanced electrical equipment, emerging bio-medicine, high-end rail infrastructure and high-tech maritime engineering.

Market economy: An economy in which goods are bought and sold and prices are determined by the free market, with a minimum of external government control. A market economy is the basis of the capitalist system.

Megacity: Metropolitan area with a total population of more than 10 million people.

Middle-income Trap: Theoretical economic development situation, in which a country that attains a certain income (due to given comparative advantages) gets stuck at that level. According to the idea, a country in the middle-income trap has lost its competitive edge in the export of manufactured goods because of rising wages. However, it is unable to keep up with more developed countries in high-value-added goods and services.

Moderate poverty: Average daily income/consumption between $1.90 and $3.10 a day (at 2015 international prices), allowing people to live just above subsistence levels. At the end of 2015, more than 1.5 billion people (World Bank figure) were living in moderate poverty across the world.

Multiplier effect: The chain reaction associated with cumulative causation. For example, the introduction of a new industry creates jobs directly in that industry, but it also creates jobs indirectly in other businesses, thereby increasing the number of times money spent circulates through the economy (local, regional or national).

Newly Industrialised Country: Country with a growing industrial economy, and a developing trade status in the global economy. Its level of economic development ranks it somewhere between the LICs and HICs.

Optimum population: The population level at which the standard of living of the people of a country or a region within a country is the highest possible relative to the level of resources and technology available.

Overpopulation: Too many people for the resources available in a country or region, therefore preventing a suitable standard of living and quality of life to be achieved. Overpopulation is likely to lead to the rapid depletion of natural resources and environmental deterioration.

Soft Power: Persuasive approach to international relations, typically involving the use of economic or cultural influence.

Sovereign wealth funds: State-owned investment funds investing in real and financial assets such as property, precious metals, bonds and stocks, or in alternative investments such as private equity funds or hedge funds. Sovereign wealth funds invest globally. Most are funded by revenues from commodity exports, or from foreign-exchange reserves held by the central bank.

Special Economic Zones: Geographical regions that have economic and other laws that are more free market orientated than a country's typical or national law. In China, these acted as doorways through for the government to attract foreign direct investment and test whether the formerly centrally-planned economy could transition to a more liberal and capitalist economy.

Spread effects: The growth of one particular area (the core) can lead to benefits for the surrounding areas (the periphery) by increasing demand for agricultural goods and raw materials, and even consumer goods industries. Spread effects are therefore positive and create regional convergence in social and economic levels of development.

Supply chain: The steps it takes to get a product or service to the customer.

Sustainability: Ensuring desirable conditions for future generations - economic, political, cultural and ecological. Sustainability occurs when living conditions and resource-use meet human needs, without undermining the sustainability of natural systems and the environment.

Technology outsourcing: A company's outsourcing of computer or internet related work, such as programming, to other companies.

Trade deficit: The amount by which the cost of a country's imports exceeds the value of its exports.

Trade surpluses: The amount, over a period of time, by which the value of a country's exports exceeds the cost of its imports.

Transnational Corporations: Companies that own or control production or services facilities in one or more countries, other than the home country. They play an important role in the process of globalisation.

Value chain: The process in which businesses receive raw materials, add value to them through production, manufacturing and other processes to create a finished product, and then sell the finished product to consumers.

World Trade Organization: Global international organisation dealing with the rules of trade between nations. The WTO has about 150 members, accounting for about 95% of world trade. At the heart of the system, known as the multilateral trading system, are the WTO's agreements, negotiated and signed by a large majority of the world's trading nations, and ratified in their parliaments. These agreements are the legal ground-rules for international commerce.

Bibliography

References and further reading:

The Economist (2019) 'The story of China's economy as told through the world's biggest building'. Available online at https://www.economist.com/essay/2019/02/23/the-story-of-chinas-economy-as-told-through-the-worlds-biggest-building

The Economist (2018) 'How the West got China wrong'. Available online at https://www.economist.com/leaders/2018/03/01/how-the-west-got-china-wrong

The Economist (2018) 'China has a vastly ambitious plan to connect the world'. Available online at https://www.economist.com/briefing/2018/07/26/china-has-a-vastly-ambitious-plan-to-connect-the-world

The Economist (2018) 'How China Made It'. Available online at https://chinafocus.economist.com/index.php/how-china-made-it/

BBC News Reports on China's Economy (2017-2020). Available online at https://www.bbc.co.uk/news/topics/cywd23g0qnmt/china-economy

Klaus Schwab (2018) 'The Global Competitiveness Report 2018', World Economic Forum. Available online at https://www.weforum.org/reports/the-global-competitveness-report-2018

Fortune Global 500 (2018). Available online at www.fortune.com/global500

Al-Atraqchi, F. (2015) '2015: The year of blaming China?', The BRICS Post. Available online at www.thebricspost.com/2015-the-year-of-blaming-china/#.VpLXBzY_k4M

Elliott, L. and Inman, P (2015) 'China syndrome: how the slowdown could spread to the Brics and beyond', The Guardian. Available online at www.theguardian.com/business/2015/aug/22/could-china-crisis-spread-to-emerging-markets

Acknowledgements

There are many people whose support, patience and guidance have helped to make my book writing exploits possible.

I would like to thank my family for their patience during the many hours of research and writing, often taking place in what was supposed to be our holiday time.

A special thanks to my son, Matt, for his expertise with spreadsheet data, enabling me to include the graphs that appear in this book.

My mother, Pat, has been a source of much inspiration and encouragement, signposting areas to research on the places and themes that appear in this book.

My late father, Michael, taught me the importance of perseverance and 'keeping the faith', advice that has helped when faced with numerous obstacles during the book writing process.

Finally, a big thank you to the Geography students that I have taught over the years, particularly those in my A Level groups at Leicester Grammar School and Wellingborough School. Their interest in my books, along with their enthusiasm for geographical learning, have been the inspiration for me to continue with my writing.

Printed in Great Britain
by Amazon